MOMENTS ALONG A TRAIL

Thomas Buzas

Photographs by Thomas Buzas.
Cover and interior design and layout by:
Somberg Design / www.sombergdesign.com

Cover photograph:
The Guillotine, Apple Orchard Mountain, Virginia

ISBN 978-0-9967404-0-1

Contents

FLYING INTO KATMAI NATIONAL PARK

Disclamations
Not all of me or only me,
this story is, in detail,
neither biographical,
but taken by empathy,
nor autobiographical,
but true expressively.
What is fact and what fantasy,
I shall never tell.
Look too closely
and you will lose the trail.

In May 2014, Susquehanna Slim and his wife took me to their home near the Appalachian Trail (AT) in an act of "Trail Magic," which is any kindness shown to a hiker. Slim had been my best friend on the AT in 2013. They helped me to resupply; fed me delicious, high-calorie, balanced meals; allowed me to shower and sleep in a warm, comfortable bed; then returned me to the Trail well rested and refreshed. We relived our adventure and renewed our friendship.

At one point, Slim said I had gotten a lot out of my experience hiking the prior year. I hadn't felt that way. Instead, I had considered myself a failure. Unlike Slim and Danno, my closest Trail friends, who had hiked the entire 2,186 miles from Springer Mountain in Georgia to Mount Katahdin in Maine, I left the Trail at Daleville, Virginia, on May 22, 2013, after 66 days and 724 miles. In July I rejoined the Trail in Connecticut, hoping to reach Katahdin with my friends, only to quit again on the second day after 18 miles. In 2014, I picked back up at Daleville, intending to hike to Connecticut, arriving in time for a wedding. This time I left the trail 40 miles short of my goal and never made it to the wedding.

My friend referred not to the miles I had covered, but how much the experience of trekking had affected me. He added that I had begun to write, had become more physically fit, and even had lost some weight—we had all lost weight on the Trail, but I had kept an extra 20 pounds off. However, Slim referred to a deeper change he observed in me.

NEAR TENNESSEE-
NORTH CAROLINA
BORDER

Every trek is a unique experience, its own story. This book tells mine. It covers the visible public experience of trekking the Appalachian Trail: the mountains, the people, the difficulties and triumphs of walking long distances in a wilderness. It also covers my private journey while walking hour after hour, day after day, often alone and deep in thought. For in addition to the story of my hikes, it reviews the nine years following my divorce in 2005 and my subsequent search for female companionship and romantic love, in particular the story of a failed romance; I proposed marriage only to break up with my fiancée on the drive home to Michigan from Alaska.

Each of the ten chapters of this book concentrates upon a stanza from the poem "Moments." Chapters One through Nine consist of two parts: the first section shares my experiences while hiking the Appalachian Trail, while the second section focuses on a stage in the evolution of a romance. In Chapter Ten, the two stories converge.

My experiences at writing about the Trail versus the story of my romance differed in a revealing manner. The text about trekking emerged easily, and I only added a few more poems over time, whereas initially I wrote many poems about romance but almost no text at all. It was difficult for me to express my emotions in prose. Instead, my poems carried the story. Only when the poems were completed was I able to go back to write the accompanying text; even then it remained challenging to write in plain words about the events.

Like a stereotypical male, I haven't always been in touch with my emotions. Sometimes, when asked how I felt about some pressing issue, I joked, "Let me get back to you on that in a couple days." It seemed that women and some men were living a much richer, more complex and conscious emotional life than I.

When I hiked, however, the physical intensity of trekking consumed all of my energy. Yet, it remained difficult for me to come to grips with my emotions until I tried to express them through poetry, thereby allowing past events and emotions to surface. Attempting to portray an event in a poem helped me to clarify the emotions associated with an experience. Also, it seemed permissible, through the magic of poetic license, to be more emotional in a poem than would be proper for a male in daily life. Interestingly, this effect held whether the event was entirely mine or borrowed from someone who had told me about an important incident in their life. In their stories, I recognized similar experiences and emotions to my own.

CROSSING THE BALDS, NORTH CAROLINA

Introduction

Come Hike with Me

Rise up! Come hike with me.
Some bright, early morning,
we'll go places you want to be,
do things you want to do,
and see sights you long to see.
Come breathe clean mountain air,
and enjoy nature's fine beauty.
Pick a day, any day. I'll be there for you.

(continued)

Why, at the age of 61, for the first time, did I go trekking? Imagine yourself being 50-something, single after 20-some years of marriage, with time for anything now that you have retired and the kids are making their own lives. You hang out with friends and find activities to keep busy. You run wild for a while but quickly tire of that. No matter how hard you may try, by nature, you are not wild. Yet, you pass through a series of relationships, none lasting very long. You have a serious relationship but that has had an unfortunate ending. You wonder whether your future will consist of a seemingly endless stream of women who will come into your life and then leave.

You feel like that awkward, insecure youth 50-some years ago, when adults would ask, "What do you want to be when you grow up?" except now the question is, "What do you want to do with the rest of your life?" A few years have gone by and you still don't have an answer.

The recent deaths of several friends also motivated me as well as what I had seen at the nursing homes where my daughters had worked during college. Occasionally, Otis, our basset hound, and I brought a meal to my daughters at work. When I observed the residents confined to the home, I resolved to make the most of my good health. I decided to make my seventh decade be my decade of adventure.

In addition to being an adventure, a trek would provide me with the opportunity to get away by myself, in a pilgrimage of sorts to experience solitude, assess my life, and to try my hand at writing poetry.

I had always been considered to be a math and science guy, not a writer. Yet, lines and fragments had been coming to me in dreams and when I was awake, emotions and thoughts wanting to be expressed. Six months on a trail seemed to offer the best opportunity for me to complete these thoughts and hopefully clear my head of these persistent percolates.

But poetry? Poetry is, after all, possibly the most artistic form of writing, and I have never been considered artistic. Apart from music, I had no appreciation for art. Partly because I had been told I had no skill at writing, possibly from conceit, and to occupy my mind while hiking, I decided to try writing poetry.

In good health, physically capable, and not taking any medications, with no scheduled weddings, graduations, births, operations, or imminent deaths in the family and being unattached, my 61st year was a good time to go on a long hike.

There were several trails for me to choose from. The 460-mile El Camino de Santiago in Spain would be a true pilgrimage from southern France to the Cathedral of Saint James in northwest Spain. The Pacific Crest Trail would provide more solitude for reflection, being more remote and less well-traveled than the Appalachian Trail. The AT had the advantages of being closer to home, having more entry and exit points, being well-documented and more popular. Because I was inexperienced, the Appalachian Trail appeared to be the safest of the three. I started researching and preparing in the fall of 2012.

There are three kinds of hikers: through-hikers plan to complete the entire Trail in one season; section hikers divide the Trail into a series of shorter hikes varying from months to weeks; and those who go out for a day or weekend, returning home or to some other facility for the night, are called day-hikers. I hoped to complete the AT in one season, but became a section hiker.

Before undertaking the AT, I consulted through-hikers but discounted their warnings as exaggeration if not braggadocio. I learned the price through-hikers paid—and it was a steep fare. Through-hiking was much harder than I could have possibly imagined. How hard? Go hike 80-90 miles in a week carrying a 35-pound backpack. Then imagine doing that for six months.

The numbers were daunting to consider, but so far beyond my experience, that they were incomprehensible. I timed myself with a full backpack; I averaged 2.25 miles per hour across mixed terrain in Michigan. At that rate, it would take almost 1,000 hours or just over two dozen 40-hour workweeks to complete the 2,186 miles of the Appalachian Trail. Rain, snow, and treacherous terrain would slow my pace, lengthening the hiking time required. Internet estimates of the elevation gained (and lost) over the AT average around 500,000 feet. Thus in addition to the miles, imagine each day climbing up and down the Washington Monument seven times or the Empire State Building three times, if some days less, other days correspondingly more. But there I go again, saying how hard the Appalachian Trail was.

But that is the difference between hiking and trekking. Go out for a day, that's hiking. Go for a weekend, that's hiking and camping. Go for a week, that's still hiking and camping. Sometime after a week, it's not hiking anymore. It's trekking. I was aware of the distinction, but did not comprehend the implications until experiencing trekking for myself.

I am not among the best of trekkers. Although I can hike the miles and am improving with each effort, I complain too much or, at least, I did in 2013. Trekking was much harder than I had imagined, and I didn't care who knew or how often.

To complete a through-hike, one needs to be strong, tough, and lucky—very lucky, because there were many good reasons to stop hiking. One friend accepted employment; others left to attend to family matters. The best reason I ever heard was from a young man who decided to enroll in summer school in order to graduate and marry the young woman with whom he was hiking. While it would be a great accomplishment to finish the Appalachian Trail, it was a far greater achievement to have realized what he valued and so he left to pursue that instead.

Some trekkers were injured. A retired military nurse never revealed the pain she was enduring. When I complimented her as "one tough lady," she replied, "You have no idea." I didn't. She hiked to Unicoi Gap, milepost 53, before she could get into Hiawassee, Georgia, reportedly to learn that she had cracked several ribs in a fall on her second day out. A young man dislocated his shoulder in the Smokies, not once but twice, the second time knocking him off-trail and putting him into physical therapy. A Trail Angel—anyone who provides Trail Magic is a "Trail Angel"—had broken his leg 80 miles from completing a through-hike. He had been air-lifted out following a miracle phone call from the dead cell zone of Maine's 100-Mile Wilderness to his wife back home. One of the strongest hikers, a fit young lady from Michigan, reportedly overdid it walking until she suffered stress fractures of both feet.

Some trekkers got sick. One friend caught Lyme disease. Near the end of May 2013, I was resting in Daleville, Virginia, milepost 724. Friends had been cautioning me about my cough, but I had dismissed their concern until I could no longer ignore the gut-wrenching hacking. They convinced me to rest a few days while I reconsidered leaving the Trail, but I decided to return home. I started taking the antibiotics I always bring with me on long journeys. Once home, a doctor refilled the prescription and added an inhaler. I had been sicker than I had suspected. It wasn't until September that I felt strong again.

I was lucky to have left the Trail when I did, perhaps much more fortunate than I had realized. On April 11, 2014, I had lunch with three southbound hikers at Seeley-Woodworth Shelter, milepost 813, in Virginia. Two were brothers, in their late fifties perhaps; the other was a young man hiking alone. The older brother joked with me about being a north-bounder. There is a good-natured rivalry between those headed north and those going south, usually over who smells worse. When I arrived in Front Royal, Virginia, on April 26, I was shocked to learn that a hiker, perhaps he, had sickened and died in a shelter a few days earlier. Might this have been my fate in 2013 if I hadn't started taking the antibiotics and headed home? More likely I would have left in worse shape than I had.

Ironically, after 700 miles of hiking in 2013, I hurt my knee on the stairs at home. An X-ray proved inconclusive. I declined an MRI because the findings would not alter the first course of treatment: rest and physical therapy. Following my release from physical therapy, I rushed back to Connecticut at the end of July, hoping to meet my friends and finish New England with them, but my knee wasn't ready for the Trail. Falling is an unfortunate but common occurrence while hiking, however, my knee kept buckling and causing me to stumble. I fell more than was normal for me until I took a short tumble down an easy incline. It is surprisingly difficult to tumble wearing a backpack, so I was shocked when I actually rolled over a couple of times.

My knee's weakness greatly concerned me, because their strength had been one of my stronger points as a hiker. Whereas other hikers would pass by me going up hills, I might catch up to them or even pass them on long downhill portions, particularly when the path was steep, uneven, or rocky. Going downhill is hard on the knees, and young hikers commented that, for an old man, I had good knees.

While sitting at the next campground, deliberating whether to proceed, my phone rang. One of my credit cards had already been cancelled due to a hacking incident at a retailer and a new one mailed to my house, where it sat useless to me. A second credit card company was calling to ask whether I had purchased a television online that morning. Now that card was cancelled and a new one mailed to my home. I was left with the cash on hand and some traveler's checks. Worse, the bills automatically paid by my credit card needed to be paid. There always is a way for the resourceful to continue, but I was fearful of reinjuring my knee, if not before, when I reached the tough mountains beginning in Vermont. My knee was street-ready but not trail-ready. Fortunately, I had left my truck with a cousin nearby. She kindly picked me up, then I drove home.

My knee healed slowly, accelerating only after I began working with a trainer. Come April 2014, I restarted the AT, for the third time, where I had left the prior year at Daleville, Virginia. My goal in 2014 was more modest. I hoped to arrive in Connecticut, almost 700 miles, in 67 days. I fared much better in 2014, only falling once when I tried to overpower a branch that had snared my foot.

LAST DAY, 2014: VIEW ACROSS NEW JERSEY AND NEW YORK

As I neared my goal, one trekking pole kept collapsing despite my repeatedly cleaning and tightening it. The other pole was bent. One boot leaked. My sleeping air pad was leaking, and I was beginning to tire of the lonely hike. Then it started to rain. It was expected to rain heavily for the next three days. I couldn't rely upon one pole; I didn't relish hiking with one foot wet nor sleeping on cold, wet ground. My options were to shelter or spend around $500 on new gear to go the remaining 40 miles. Even though I was ten days early, I had accomplished enough for 2014. At the next town I enjoyed first a pizza and a beer, then a BBQ dinner with coffee while waiting for a car rental company to pick me up.

During the drive to the rental center to fill out the paperwork, I felt an irritation on my back when I leaned against the car seat. Looking in a bathroom mirror, I saw there a large red swelling. *Not going to get better on its own*, I thought. I started taking my antibiotics and went to a doctor when I got home. He did what was necessary and advised me to continue taking the antibiotic while waiting for test results. Laboratory testing confirmed MRSA, a form of staph resistant to antibiotics. As luck would have it, that particular strain was sensitive to the antibiotic I was already taking. I didn't think much more about the matter until a follow-up visit when they directed me to a special entrance where a nurse wearing a mask, eye-covering, gloves, and gown greeted me. MRSA is highly contagious and dangerous. In order not to cause any anxiety among the wedding party and guests, I called to explain that I would be unable to attend.

Fortunately, the infection cleared up in a few weeks. Skin irritations were a perpetual threat on the Trail due to trekkers being constantly wet from either sweat or rain, but I had been exposed to the MRSA bacteria somewhere off-trail. It had been waiting for an opportunity to infect a scratch or scrape. Thankfully, there has been no indication that I harbor MRSA chronically.

Recently, a through-hiker friend has suggested that I am well in tune with my body, instinctively knowing when to temporarily retire from the quest. Then again, maybe I am just lucky. I'll take lucky.

While I hope to complete the Trail someday, forgive me if I ponder the necessity as I approach my 64th birthday. But, you know my decision: I will return. Because far from being a miserable experience, trekking is exhilarating, and I was gloriously happy most of the time. More than once others commented on my big smile. Almost every day is wonderful.

Come Hike with me (continued)
Come, my dear, walk with me.
Feel my breath upon your cheek.
Smell my familiar scents.
Be bold, my love, not meek.
Ascend my steep ascents.

Rest here upon these peaks
Descend my deep descents.
Come now. Sleep with me
and find the peace you seek.
(continued)

⁂

Oh, I do become a cranky old man when people intrude upon my space and when I become stressed. In 2014, I was content seeing one or two people and rarely sharing a shelter or campsite until into May. I am happiest sharing meals and talking into the night with a few people rather than with a crowd. I have made a number of good trail friends this way, friends with whom I remain in contact, and that is enough for me.

Sometimes I joked that one of the nicest aspects to the Trail was that I was able to make friends with men and women of all types and ages. Out in the world, young men and women might wonder what this old pervert was after, while I would be wondering whether they were planning to rob me. Being around the same people time and again, friendships developed naturally.

Several of my Appalachian Trail friends had been young men and women. I called three of these young ladies "my trail daughters" to alleviate any anxiety about my friendliness and intentions. Olive Oyl was tall and thin with an olive complexion, resembling the character from the comic strip "Popeye." She was soft-spoken and witty. Candy Pants was cheerfully perky. She wore pants adorned with images of candies. I inadvertently gave Lady her trail name at Low Gap Shelter, milepost 41, in Georgia, when I wished her and a shelter full of would-be suitors, "Good night, Lady and Bums." She said no one had ever called her a lady before, but at least when she was around me, she was straight-talking and stately in bearing.

Two of the young ladies sang. Besides being entertaining, their singing endeared them to me. They sang at random happy times. Either might sing softly in her tent at night or in the morning. One sang while washing dishes, the other while brushing her hair. After I told one I enjoyed her singing, she sang her side of a conversation instead of speaking with me. How much I treasured their singing! How much I wished these youths would enjoy all the best that life has to offer and find true love.

My wishes for my trail daughters and for my own children made me think about my past failed romantic relationships. "Failed" might be too strong of a word, but "over" or "ended" would be too weak.

Outside Pearisburg, Virginia, one beautiful, sunny yet brutally hot day with a strong drying wind, I had lunch with Lady and HoBo, a man approaching retirement age who was Homeward Bound to Maine. We were slack-packing back into town with Dreamer, a man slightly younger than me, who was also from Michigan. We lost track of Dreamer, because he was stopping to film his hike. He edited and posted the films online. (They were very well done.) By the way, slack-packing means we were hiking with a day pack while our full packs remained back in Pearisburg.

Lady, HoBo, and I met for lunch. While we lingered over our meal of local cheeses and freshly baked bread, we shared true stories of romances we had known. That was the day I began work on the poem, "Moments," which provides the framework for this book.

"Moments" presents my thoughts about the stages in a romantic relationship. I came to these observations from three directions: the first, from reflecting on my own life and loves; the second, from thinking about lasting relationships I had observed; and the third, from the experience of trekking. In particular, while I reflected on my life, I noticed similarities and differences between my past romantic relationships and the current experience of trekking.

Moments

Might this be love
in its first golden moment,
or just a moment
that, having passed,
will end in disappointment
and embarrassment?

What if not love,
but only a delirium
of passion carried
by enthusiasm
until it collapses,
momentum spent?

Or just a game,
like careless children pretending,
a game each too kind to end,
or still playing
to avoid blame for ending
a game gone errant?

Could we be fools,
like anxious adolescents,
wanting to believe
in love constant,
and thus eager accomplices
to our ensnarement?

Although not a trick,
more like an arrangement:
each needing the other
to a precious purpose,
but once accomplished,
then to what end, commitment?

A last habit,
like old folks feeling frail
avoiding risk,
forgoing excitement,
settling for familiarity
and contentment.

If, of these, none,
neither love idyllic
nor moment vanishing,
not a habit, trick,
game or understanding,
what is left then but sentiment?

A lasting gift
that cannot be purchased,
only given,
sometimes squandered,
often neglected or forgotten,
and yet persistent.

What if all,
not one or none, but each and every,
and more unspoken
or imagined,
ten thousand moments to love or end,
might that be love?

A mystery,
a secret hidden from all
but its participants,
yet recognized
as present or absent
by the observant.

I BEGAN THE TRAIL AT AMICALOLA STATE PARK, GEORGIA, WHERE I CLIMBED THE STAIRS BESIDE
THE BEAUTIFULLY CASCADING FALLS.

CHAPTER 1: *Anticipation*

Might this be love
in its first golden moment,
or just a moment
that, having passed,
will end in disappointment
and embarrassment?

THE BEGINNING

Come Hike with Me (continued)
Come, follow me to Georgia,
where one mild mid-March morning,
we'll climb the stairs at Amicalola,
stop at the last restroom,
cross the parking lot,
and start the Trail through Appalachia.

My preparations for the Trail including reading books written by through-hikers and survivalists with TV shows and studying maps and guides to the Appalachian Trail. The nephew of one of my friends was a through-hiker and his wife had joined him for the last half of the Trail. They were kind enough to share stories and advice.

My daughters expressed concern about my safety, but we have a deal. As they grew older, if they wanted me to support their decisions financially and emotionally, they had to listen to my opinion beforehand. It would remain their decision, but because they had taken time and gathered information, I would support their final choice. Conversely, if they acted without soliciting my input, I might not support their decision.

Now they applied that same rule to me. Both are health care workers, and inspected my treatments for illnesses and injuries. I had already completed a 3-day Wilderness First Aid course offered through Recreational Sports at the University of Michigan. My med kit included two prescription antibiotics:

one to treat intestinal distress and the other for tick-borne diseases, as well as an assortment of over-the-counter pills and a mixture of bandages and salves. They then made me to promise to leave the Trail if I ever felt at risk. Satisfied, they agreed to mail packages to resupply points along the Trail. These packages would contain homemade dehydrated meals and other foods, maps of the upcoming section of the AT, additional items I called to request, a few surprise treats, and notes expressing their pride, support, and love.

At Christmas of 2012, before starting the Trail, I showed my backpack and its contents to my brothers, nephews, and, especially, to my mother. Although they remained concerned for my safety, they seemed convinced that I had thought this through.

My daughters organized a send-off party. My ex-wife and her significant other attended. Afterward, my daughters gave me letters to read after I started the Trail. These letters would make me cry.

My younger daughter and a friend drove me to the southern starting point of the Trail. At daybreak on March 15, 2013, they dropped me off at the Visitors Center at Amicalola State Park, Georgia. We took pictures, then said our good-byes, with hugs, kisses, and apprehension. It would be the longest period we had ever been apart. I am fortunate to have two devoted daughters who live near me. We get together most weeks, sometimes more than once.

At 7 a.m., I signed the trail register for through-hikers at the Visitor Center. Mine was about the 400th entry. Then I began to climb the stairs alongside the beautifully cascading 729-foot Amicalola Falls to begin the Approach Trail. The southern terminus of the Appalachian Trail at Springer Mountain was 8.8 miles north of Amicalola across the first three mountains, Amicalola, Black, and Springer. Some trekkers choose to begin the Appalachian Trail at a small parking lot a mile north of Springer Mountain, then walk south to the official starting point of the AT before turning around and walking north. Others start from a nearby inn, about 5 miles off the Approach Trail. Because I wanted to experience everything about the AT, I started at Amicalola.

I began with feelings of anxious exhilaration and hopeful anticipation. What adventures lay ahead? Whom would I meet? Would I make friends? Would I make it safely to the end of the Trail in Maine at Mount Katahdin?

I met my first trail friends, Cruise and Corn Dog, when we ascended Springer Mountain together. I thought Cruise was named because of her steady pace, but the name had familial significance. Corn Dog was fond of corny jokes. They were not typical hikers, being married and more mature than the majority of youthful hikers. We met often along the Trail, each time a more joyful reunion, and each time they grew dearer to me. In suitable closure to my hike in 2013, Cruise and Corn Dog would be the last people I saw on the Trail when I decided to get off at Daleville nine weeks later. During my 2014 hike, they sent me encouraging messages and videos.

APPALACHIA

Appalachia.
    Say it again.
Appalachia.
    When you say it,
"Appalachia?"
    it sounds like a prayer.

Where did you begin?	*Step by step*
Amicalola.	*onto Katahdin.*
Where is that?	*Step by step*
Down south in Georgia.	*onto Katahdin.*
What was next?	
Tennessee	*Step by step*
and North Carolina,	*onto Katahdin.*
Virginia	*Step by step*
and West Virginia,	*onto Katahdin;*
Maryland	*Step by step*
and Pennsylvania,	*onto Katahdin;*
New Jersey	*Step by step,*
and New York.	*We're not there yet.*
We're not there yet.	

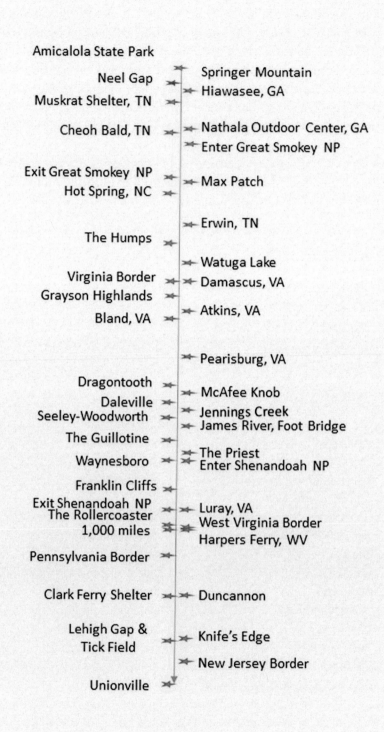

Amicalola State Park
Neel Gap — Springer Mountain
Muskrat Shelter, TN — Hiawasee, GA

Cheoh Bald, TN — Nathala Outdoor Center, GA
— Enter Great Smokey NP

Exit Great Smokey NP
Hot Spring, NC — Max Patch

— Erwin, TN
The Humps

— Watuga Lake
Virginia Border — Damascus, VA
Grayson Highlands
Bland, VA — Atkins, VA

— Pearisburg, VA

Dragontooth — McAfee Knob
Daleville — Jennings Creek
Seeley-Woodworth — James River, Foot Bridge
The Guillotine
Waynesboro — The Priest
Enter Shenandoah NP
Franklin Cliffs
Exit Shenandoah NP — Luray, VA
The Rollercoaster — West Virginia Border
1,000 miles — Harpers Ferry, WV

Pennsylvania Border

Clark Ferry Shelter — Duncannon

Lehigh Gap &
Tick Field — Knife's Edge
— New Jersey Border
Unionville

SEE ALSO: APPALACHIAN NATIONAL SCENIC TRAIL OFFICIAL BROCHURE MAP
http://www.nps.gov/appa/planyoaurvisit/brochures.htm

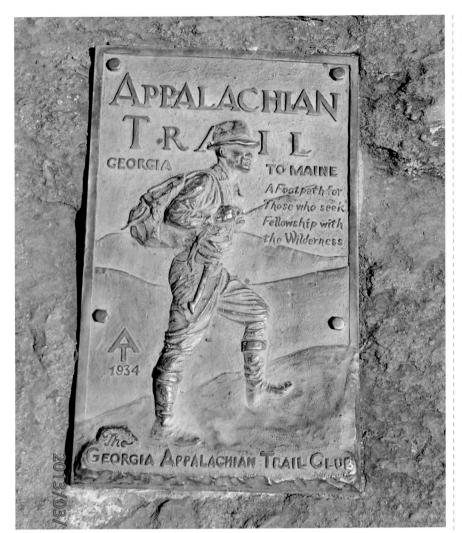

Around 1 p.m., I reached the top of Springer and noted that I was proceeding more slowly than expected, only 1.5 miles per hour. I took a
picture of the plaque marking the start of the Appalachian Trail. It read:
"Appalachian Trail, Georgia to Maine: A Footpath for Those who seek
Fellowship with the Wilderness, 1934, The Georgia Appalachian Trail Club,"
then looked around for the first of the many famous white blazes that marked
the Trail. Trails are marked by cairns, rocks assembled in small towers, but
usually by blazes painted on trees, rocks, fences, railways, underpasses, even
on roads and sidewalks. Vertical white stripes identified the Appalachian
Trail. Different colors differentiated trails intersecting the AT. Side trails,
such as to water or optional trails around dangerous sections, were marked by
blue colors. In the game lands of Pennsylvania, additional large white stripes
were painted on trees facing toward the Trail from each side warning hunters
not to shoot across the Trail.

At Springer, a trail runner paid by the Appalachian Conservancy to watch out for the Trail and through-hikers advised spending the night there because the campgrounds and shelters ahead were already crowded. That weekend had brought the first nice spring-like weather to Georgia. Through-hikers, families, church groups, scouts, and others crowded the trails. The noise and bustle reminded me of a street fair.

It was difficult to follow her advice to camp at Springer for my first night on the Trail. The weather was perfect. I was eager, well rested, and had trained, working up to 50 miles a week while wearing my fully loaded backpack back in the flatlands of Michigan. My body was restlessly urging me on. Resisting my desire to continue, I spent the first night at Springer.

Going slowly had been great advice. Estimates range widely, but the staff at the outfitter in Neel Gap said that around 20 percent of those attempting a through-hike have ended their quest by the time they reach the store at milepost 31. Businesses try to keep track of the numbers and pass that information along to other businesses further up the Trail, but no one really knows the exact numbers. In 2015, the Appalachian Trail Conservancy instituted an online registration system to help manage the Trail. Distances are measured from the plaque at Springer for those headed north and from Katahdin in Maine for those heading south. Mileposts are approximate, because the distances change due to rerouting that occurs every year.

During the next few days I passed overeager hikers stuck at their campsites suffering from blisters, muscle aches, and injuries. Going too far too fast at the beginning in 2013 would have been a terrible mistake for me.

Although I had trained, I wasn't ready to trek. Back home after hiking, I would enjoy a shower, town food, and all of the comforts of civilization. One adjusts slowly to trail life: taking sponge baths using biodegradable wipes or cold stream water, eating camp food, digging cat holes, and getting by without the casual luxuries and conveniences of home.

Trekkers talk about waiting to get your "mountain legs," but in my case, I think it is more accurate to talk about getting my "trail feet." My legs were ready long before my feet. It took a few weeks to build the strength in my feet and ankles and to develop the calluses needed to cover the distances demanded.

Feet endure a terrible pounding while trekking. Even a small blister can and has become a major problem for me. Not until it feels like my feet are wearing gloves are they truly ready. Even then, trekking is always about the feet.

In addition, I have an unresolved issue with boots: my left foot is a full size larger than the right foot. I could purchase two pairs of boots, one fitting my left foot and the other, my right, wearing one boot from each pair. Instead I buy to fit my left foot, allowing extra room to accommodate the swelling that will occur. I make do by lacing my right boot extra tightly and wearing sock liners to reduce the blisters that might develop from my right foot sliding back and forth inside its oversized boot.

Hiking with a 35-pound backpack must be a little like being pregnant, with the mother's feet growing larger and more swollen over time. Hikers treat their swollen feet by resting with them elevated, soaking them in cold streams, and by consuming massive quantities of "vitamin I," more commonly known as ibuprofen. Once my feet toughened up, I didn't need the ibuprofen and my knees never bothered me. If it was going to be a rough day, I might take a pill or two in the morning or, if it had been a tough day, at night, but most days I didn't take any at all.

TRAIL TERMS

Blaze – a painted stripe marking a trail or side trail

Blue blaze – a blaze marking a side trail, usually to water

Hostel – a community sleeping facility ranging from a bunkhouse to semi-private rooms

Nearo – a day with a little hiking

Rule of Three – a survivalist saying: you can survive three minutes without air, three hours without shelter, three days without water, three weeks without food.

Slack-packing – hiking without your full pack. A trekker may send their full pack ahead or be hiking back to where they have left their pack, such as at a lodging or outfitter.

Trail Angel – anyone who provides Trail Magic

Trail Magic – any act of kindness toward a trekker by a non-trekker

Trail name – the name you use when you hike

White blaze – blaze marking the Appalachian Trail

Vitamin I – ibuprofen

Zero – a day with no hiking

While staying at Springer, I enjoyed listening to the trail-runner's stories about her through-hike with her engineer husband.

Sooner or later though, I stubbed my toes thereby blackening the toenails on my left foot. Following the hiking season, these toenails slowly fell off while the hard-earned calluses peeled away in thick, leathery strips. My feet may be hardy, but they are ugly.

During the first weeks, 10–12 miles is a full day of hiking. As your feet and legs strengthen, you finish that distance earlier in the day. Because it is too early to stop for the night, you continue further. In this manner, your mileage naturally increases from 10 miles to 12, then 14, 16, until you are able to do 20 miles or more on some days.

One of the best pieces of advice was from an old-timer who had completed multiple through-hikes. We sat at the dinner table in one of my favorite hostels run by a colorful character in Damascus, Virginia. The veteran trekker advised taking my "zeros" on the Trail. Rest days are called a "zero" because you travel "zero" miles and "nearo" when you hike only a few miles. He pointed out that in town, I was constantly running around doing errands whereas on the trail, there wasn't anything to do but eat and rest, talk, read, and write.

Belatedly, in 2014, I took his advice, which proved most beneficial. In addition, I took longer breaks, two or three "zeros" in a row, whereas in 2013, I usually took only one zero at a time before hurrying back to the trail. The extra day or two of rest helped tremendously, but only if I really spent the time resting. This meant I had to carry extra food when I left town; yet each time I diligently rested, I returned to hiking noticeably stronger with a marked uptick in my daily mileage thereafter.

Over the first month of hiking in 2013, I had averaged 65 miles per week versus 85 miles per week over the rest of my hike. In 2014, I slowed my pace, never doing more than 14 miles on any day during the first month and averaged a lowly 56 miles per week for those first four weeks, but for the remainder of 2014, I averaged 94 miles per week.

While staying at Springer, I enjoyed listening to the trail-runner's stories about her through-hike with her engineer husband. To pass the time, they had constructed humorously pithy "Trail Theorems," such as "When in doubt, go up." Spending so much time at Springer, I met many hikers I would see again in the days ahead. I also met two whom I did not meet again.

Bear Claw Pendant

They were at the shelter when we met.
Johnny was a good old boy,
gray and grizzled as one can get.
Joey was his grandson
fair-haired, unblemished, and innocent.

Johnny and I talked about retirement,
and things old men talk about:
family, health, taxes, and government.
I asked about the trail ahead:
"Would my preparations be adequate?"

When Joey spoke softly,
Johnny helped him off to their tent.
It was then I saw the hand-carved cane,
a small plastic bear
and a real bear claw pendants.

I thought of the effort they had spent
on the mile from the parking lot.
But Johnny loved Joey,
Joey loved the mountains,
so off to the mountain they went.

I wondered what must they have thought—
had they even noticed?—
the stories of miles to be conquered
from those the mountains had not humbled,
well, at least not yet.

I've thought of the days before we met,
and all the days since,
and a burden carried without complaint or credit
until one day that weight will be lifted
and a longer, harder journey ended.

When I complain about things
that shame me to admit,
sometimes I remember a cheerful boy,
a small toy bear
and a real bear claw pendant.

On the second day, I received my trail name, "Apa" (pronounced "aw-pa" and accented on the first syllable), which is Hungarian for "father." Long hikers use a trail name because, while there may be a dozen guys named "Tom" hiking, your trail name may be unique. Some trail names do tend to be more common, such as "Spider." Most mornings, the lead hikers wave their hiking poles in the air before themselves hoping to clear paths through the silken spider threads floating across the trail. In one of nature's more harmless pranks, a leader is netted by the spiders, a sensation remarkably similar to a wakening splash of icy cold water to the face, and in testimony to their reaction, receive the trail name of "Spider."

Some trekkers chose their own trail name, although to me this seems to be denying themselves an essential part of the experience. True, it might be risky letting someone name you. Should you receive a trail name you didn't like, you could always refuse it or trade up a little farther down the trail. One fellow changed his name three times while I knew him. I myself was offered two other names, "Mayor" because it seemed to Danno that I knew more hikers than anyone—I stop to speak with almost everyone—and "Poet" because I was reciting my poetry to some. But I stuck with my first name because "Mayor" seemed too arrogant and my portfolio was too thin to support a claim to "Poet." I admit "Apa" was arrogant if obscurely so; there were many men hiking who deserved the designation of "father."

A ROTC marine named me "Apa" on my second day at Hawk Mountain Shelter, milepost 7.6, where we had stopped for lunch. He was listening to my conversation with another hiker who had asked what I had done before retiring. I had worked from home for 15 years. My own father was from a family of 12 children and grew up during the Great Depression. He dedicated his life to ensuring his children never went to bed hungry and that we had the opportunities he never had. He was a good provider and I am grateful to him, in particular for my education. However, we were not close. Late in life, he admitted that he had missed a lot. I wanted to be more involved with my children, who were "latchkey" kids while I traveled for business. I became a stay-at-home analyst—so to speak, the factory—supporting consultants who traveled, obtained, and managed clients. They provided sales, customer service, and so forth. I drove my daughters to school in the morning, was there when they and their friends came home in the afternoon—all of their mothers worked. Usually I took them to dance class or elsewhere. This story impressed a young man listening nearby. He asked about my ethnic background, leading to my trail name, "Apa." Bystanders seconded the nomination, and I accepted.

Since my christening, I have been told that "Apa" is also "baby talk" for father in Korea, confirmed at Mt. Collins Shelter in Tennessee, at milepost 199, by a Korean lady hiking in memory of her husband, who had always wanted to hike the trail. To my chagrin, Americans who had spent time in

Korea said that a young Korean lady might address an unrelated older man thusly, as in "sugar daddy." Recently I was told about "Apa Sherpa," a guide in Nepal who has summited Mt. Everest more than anyone else, 21 times.

Naming

At birth, we are given a name
chosen after careful deliberation,
perhaps in memory of a loved one,
or in accordance with familial tradition,
sometimes in hope revealed by its meaning,
for its sound or some other consideration
by those who have born us but do not know us.

While living, we earn a name:
by the things we do and those we leave undone,
by friends we keep and those we abandon,
by what we do for money and what we do for fun,
all the choices we make both good and bad
revealing our character and disposition.
How much better that we should be named then.

STARTING OVER

My then-wife had supported my decision to work from home. I earned enough, although there were some lean years after the attack on the World Trade Towers on September 11, 2001. I could not have worked from home for long without her continuing to support my decision and the support of my business associates, for which I am grateful. I worked from home until retiring at the end of 2011 when my youngest child completed college.

By mutual agreement, my ex-wife and I divorced rather amicably in 2005. Despite efforts, we had grown apart and agreed to seek happiness elsewhere. After the divorce, I waited until my youngest child entered college before deciding to make up for lost time. I didn't want to jump into a relationship too quickly. Others had warned me about rebound relationships, which almost never ended well. Also I wasn't sure what I wanted. Did I want a serious, ongoing relationship or just occasional companionship?

After three decades years of not dating, I didn't know what to expect. One hears many disturbing stories about mid-life dating, especially about desperate, calculating women (and men) looking for financial rescue and casual sex among the older crowd.

Moreover, I had always been somewhat clueless and naïve in social settings. During a business trip to Florida, after my divorce, I unintentionally

It might seem wonderful to start over with a clean slate. By the age of 50, however, your slate has been written upon, heavily so.

flirted with a young Caribbean receptionist at a hotel check-in, then asked her about the visiting hours at the nearby fort. "Good," I said, "I'm free that afternoon." When I arrived at the fort, I was surprised to see the receptionist. We toured the fort together. When I asked what had led her to the States, she explained, "If you never take a chance, you never have a life." Later when I told my business associate what I had done with my free time, he suggested that I had led her on. His wife, who had joined him for the weekend, only said, "Green card." My colleague asked whether I really thought the receptionist hadn't been to the fort before. None of these possibilities had entered my mind. I remain oblivious to this day, sometimes saying things without realizing how others might interpret them. My daughters collect these clueless sayings, calling them "Dadisms."

It might seem wonderful to start over with a clean slate. By the age of 50, however, your slate has been written upon, heavily so. You may have children, commitments to elderly parents, health issues, interests, plans, goals, and financial assets to protect. It's a lot different from when you were 20-something hoping to make a life with someone. At 50-something I already had a life, and so would she.

Thus relatively naive and somewhat uncertain, I started slowly. Before allowing myself to get involved and curious to see what was out there, I joined a trio of online dating services and set a goal of meeting 50 women, a joke that actually came true. I didn't keep count after 30 women but quickly met many more. My mother was happy to see me dating. Once, after I told her I was having lunch with one woman and dinner with another, she looked at my sister-in-law and gave two thumbs-up.

At first, I only wanted to have an enjoyable evening with the females I met through the websites. We compared notes about online dating. Women said men lied about their age and height. Sometimes the women were targeted by men who had fallen madly in love with them, but needed a little money due to a family emergency while he was traveling or for his business. The specific need varied, but an import business seemed to be a common factor. Everything would be wonderful, if only she could help him get a shipment through customs by fronting a few thousand dollars. Just provide her banking information and he would take care of the rest.

My experience was that women posted pictures of their younger, thinner selves. Some posted suggestive pictures of themselves reclining on a bed or beach or dressed in revealing clothing. Young women offered to send me pictures of themselves—were they even women?—if I provided my contact information. Some stated they would be my caretaker when the time came. I wasn't sure what to make of that, but it did make me feel old.

Once I sorted through the scams, I found lots of women willing to talk on the phone and, if that went well, meet in person. Mostly we quickly realized we had no interest in each other and cordially wished each other good luck and moved on with nothing more ever happening.

Sometimes we continued our conversation over dinner or a drink. If the weather was good and skies clear, we went for a ride in my sports car with the top down. Usually we called it a night, agreeing to talk later over the phone.

A few times we went back to my place or to hers. I thought, *Let's see how much things have changed in 30 years.* We started with coffee or a glass of wine, sometimes followed by a light make-out session. Several women allowed me to go further. If I crossed lines, I always respected their limits and stopped when asked. The women who resisted my advances, but still wanted to play, surprised me. *Was this to be expected?* I wondered.

I discovered I had limits of my own. Besides, there were other women to meet and, considering the proliferation of sexually transmitted diseases among older adults, I was in no hurry. Better to call it a night than to get into a more complicated situation.

When I hesitated, some women asserted themselves, or realizing they had been judged and had in some way failed, reacted angrily. When I declined one woman, she asked, "If not now, then when?" and then added, "You're not getting any younger." Another admitted she didn't want the whole pig, just some sausage now and then. Her words struck me as an odd mixture of insult and invitation. Regardless, I didn't want a woman so quick and easy to have.

One or the other, on some nights I suspect, both of us, left shaking our heads. None of these interactions proceeded further. Although the final lines were never crossed, these meetings felt like one-night stands.

Over the next few years, I was shocked by wild women. Two different women, we had only spoken on the phone, woke me in the middle of the night, inviting me to their houses, and then begging, would I please "talk" to them until they could fall sleep. *Was this for real or was it a set up?* These women and the risk they might present to my health and the potential drama associated with someone who might be emotionally or mentally unstable, frightened me.

Other times, I wasn't sure what to think. Two women, one of whom I knew, approached me at a restaurant after my daughters left and said they were looking to have some fun. I had other plans, but still wonder what they had in mind. Afterward, I thought, *Am I getting a reputation?*

I discovered I carried more emotional baggage than I had realized.

Some friends and acquaintances appeared to be living vicariously through me: they seemed to think I was having a much better time than I actually was. They would ask, "How many dates did you have this week?" or, hoping for details, "You must meet some crazy women." People seemed to assume that having a lot of dates implied promiscuity. I remembered the popular girls in high school about whom rumors floated. When someone pressed further, I would respond, "Everyone," then pause for effect, "deserves to get lucky once a year." There was much more smoke than fire.

Some situations had always seemed to be too much trouble. A woman might be in or just out of bankruptcy. She might ask whether I had health insurance. While I enjoyed a glass of wine with dinner, she finished the bottle. A member of her family might be in or just out of rehab, if not jail. While I felt sorry for the good women raising their grandchildren, I didn't want the responsibility of bringing up another generation. Some women had been married three or four times. Every family has challenges, but I had no desire to add any to mine.

Then there were the horns of politics and religion. By our ages, political and religious beliefs were firmly set. Most of the time, women were respectful about these issues; they would state that they couldn't date me because of the difference between our beliefs. A few criticized my beliefs. At times I pushed back against criticism because I did enjoy a good debate, *er* argument. These discussions never ended satisfactorily. It was much easier to change topics and then never contact them again.

I discovered I carried more emotional baggage than I had realized. There seemed to be a period when one easily confuses the new man or woman with one's ex-spouse. Something rubbed one of us the wrong way because of past associations. I was accused of saying or doing things I hadn't. I don't think I ever did that, but I definitely noted similarities to my ex-wife, things that had annoyed me and still do, if less so now. I learned to stay away from the newly divorced because they were working through their conflicting emotions of relief, loneliness, anger, and disappointment.

Family or children might interfere. Adult children still living with their mother saw me as a threat to their situation. Sometimes I simply didn't like her children, or they didn't like me.

Some women didn't want to complicate matters by involving friends or family, carefully shielding their lives from me. Although I appreciated not wanting to merge lives too quickly, I was suspicious of women who arranged our schedules to avoid any interaction with her friends and family, making me wonder whether they were hiding something, perhaps even juggling suitors. It was much less suspicious if meetings were allowed to happen naturally, for instance if I were to arrive while a friend was leaving.

Finally, I started to date one woman exclusively. I thought I was being clear about my disinclination to enter into a serious relationship quickly. Yet, I disappointed her. She wanted more commitment than I was ready to give, which led to an uncomfortable conversation.

You Had to Know

You knew I was just starting over.
I mean, you had to know
all I wanted was to have some fun.
I didn't hide it from anyone.

Now you keep coming around,
when you have nothing better to do,
and calling me on the telephone,
asking when can you see me again.

I don't want to be cruel,
but I'm not in love with you.
I wasn't playing you for a fool,
I just don't want to be with anyone.

Over the next four years, I passed through a series of gradually lengthening relationships, punctuated by periods when I did not date at all, until one day I would decide I needed to get out more and then start the cycle of phone calls and meetings again, each iteration becoming more selective about whom I would meet and date.

Surprisingly, one thing began to annoy me. There seemed to be an expectation of sex by a prescribed point, as if we were following a script. Having sex too soon proved counterproductive to establishing a lasting relationship. At some point, one of us would roll over asking ourselves, *Who the hell is this person in bed next to me?*

Yet, it was hard to resist the allure of sex. We both missed the sex. Women told me so, sometimes with a conflicted twinge in their voices, as if to say, "I shouldn't, but I *really* do want to have sex." When I heard those words in that tone, I felt trapped. I knew, *Later she will regret moving so* quickly. *Should I risk offending her by stopping? Has she already made up her mind to break up, and was just taking advantage of an opportunity?* No matter what I did, the trajectory of that relationship would be downward. It felt strange to have become the one trying to slow things down, but sooner or later, there would be an invitation to have dinner at her place. Navigating that night and afterward was tricky. *Did she only want a relaxing evening, perhaps to watch some TV or a movie, or did she expect more?*

Accidently, I discovered a way to discern a woman's intentions. Before that dinner, I would say that I was growing more attached to her. If that frightened her off, she only wanted companionship, and maybe to have sex once in a while. If she continued to see me, she remained open to a potentially more serious relationship.

Sometimes, however, I felt that I was being manipulated by sex. It saddened me to think a woman was following a timetable in the hope that it might lead to something more. Once, a woman who had never married told me she had been too good during her youth. Had it always been this way for women? I wondered what a woman might be thinking when she woke up next to me.

Waking

While you lie sleeping,
the moonlight alters your appearance,
purifying your countenance until flawless
and shining with angelic luminance
like a perfectly polished cherub puppet.

With the moonlight waning,
colors fade and shadows lengthen
until your face resembles the surface
of the moon, flat and ashen,
lined and whited, like an imprint from a woodcut.

Hurry morning,
so I can see, in your light's first virgin clarity,
his face with its waking honesty,
telling whether romance, tragicomedy,
or a play in one act consummate.

Am I seduced for dreaming?
Perhaps I have let things move too fast,
only to add another page to my storied past.
Yet, I feel, much more than hope
that this time, with this one, it just might last.

This seems so right and I, safe and secure,
I almost feel like singing,
If I were to sing softly, trying not to wake him,
would he dream of an angel singing,
then waking, discover me?

Or, should I just go back to bed,
pull back the covers and wake him instead,
make hot coffee and a warm breakfast bread,
be content not knowing yet
and of dreams remain silent?

Each time I backslid, I started again with greater resolve. I still didn't know what I was looking for, but knew more quickly when it wasn't there.

One day, I found a necklace hanging on a plant stand in my dining room. Unbeknownst to me, a woman had hung it there before we moved to a "more comfortable" location, then forgotten about it. *Whose was it?* I wondered and set it aside should someone ask for it; then forgot about it. Over the years, I accumulated a small collection of jewelry and clothing, including of all things, socks, which I donated to charity.

It was only a matter of time until my daughters confronted me about my series of affairs. It started when the daughter playing "good cop" innocently inquired, "Dad, are there any brothers or sisters we should know about?" The bad-cop daughter was more direct. We are blunt with each other. I stopped dating while I assessed what I was doing and the example I was setting.

Yes, I had met a lot of women, dated some of them, and, over four years, developed a number of relationships, each lasting from a few to several months. They all had been relationships of a sort, or at least, good-faith efforts at establishing a relationship. Sure, I could be had, but I was not that easy. Yet, I must admit that the true number of partners was larger than I would have liked. Even if slowly, year by year, the numbers do add up. After a few years, I had started to construct quite the disreputable resume. This didn't sit well with me. This wasn't what I wanted. I questioned myself, *Would good enough for now be good enough forever?*

When I began dating again, I was looking for a committed relationship I met and dated far fewer women. If the path seems clear to me now, it was not at the time. The route I had followed was confused and uncertain with many foolish missteps and mistakes. Unlike Sisyphus pushing his recalcitrant rock up a hill, I was moving forward, if not neatly so. It is hard to find someone with whom to have a successful, serious relationship at any age. It seemed harder now without the goal of starting a family together.

Each time I backslid, I started again with greater resolve. I still didn't know what I was looking for, but knew more quickly when it wasn't there.

As I focused upon finding, if not the "right" woman, at least a good fit, I became more open with women. I told them about my past, that it was behind me, and what I was looking for in the future. Sometimes they asked questions, which I answered truthfully. One woman even called me "authentic."

In response to my candor, women opened up to me about themselves. A few, during our first meeting, shared intimate details of their own lives. I heard the circumstances of their troubled upbringing, issues with their families, health concerns, the stories of their divorces and failed romantic relationships. Several told me about the difficulty of recovering from the financial ruin caused by their divorce. There were stories of neglect, infidelity, substance abuse, and worse, much worse. It was hard to listen to the heartache in their voices.

Just a Little Lie
It was just a little lie
that grew and grew
until it metastasized
and multiplied.

All the lies I told for you,
when everyone knew:
you were being untrue
and I was being a fool.

I pretended not to care,
closing my eyes,
never asking about your affairs
and alibis.

That was what I had to do.
Yes, I was sure.
I was so in love with you,
I had to endure.

I thought life would get better,
that you would stop.
You had to know
what you were doing.

But it never did get better.
I was just a prop
in your daily show
and you were only acting.

I refused to believe
you could be so cruel.
I never thought I could leave.
How does it feel now to be the fool?

Was there ever anything
in that heart of yours?
How many lies must it take
to cover a hole?

What a wonderful opportunity for a cad to take advantage of the moment. Listening to these women, however, made it impossible for me to consider being insincere. Casual intimacy would prove me a liar and violate the trust that had been established between us. We might talk or meet again but we had become too personal too quickly. Whereas becoming sexually intimate hindered development of the personal aspects of a relationship, it seemed that opening up too quickly interfered with developing a sexual relationship. A more balanced approach was needed.

No one stood out for me. The online dating profiles had taken on a certain sameness, as if they had been written by the same person. Only the pictures differed. There was something that I was not finding. I asked myself, *What am I looking for? Am I only finding excuses to avoid commitment?* And, *What about me might stand out?*

My daughters say I live in a different world, thinking and looking at things in an unusual way. I have always sought experiences rather than money, fame, power, or material possessions. I am part nerd, but worked in a foundry and a factory when I was young, briefly studied martial arts, and like to shoot. Yet, I am highly educated, have been a tenure track professor, helped start two businesses, worked with people around the world, and even attended a dinner party in a former castle. A rich and varied life has taught me to appreciate the fancy and fine but to prefer a simple and unassuming life. Although I am comfortable in varied locations, from the part of western and central Pennsylvania called Pennsyltucky to more cultured places, I have tastes, interests, and beliefs that don't fit easily into the comfort zone of academia, liberal towns, or conservative country.

She would have to be an unusual woman to appreciate and tolerate my complexities, contradictions, and eccentricities. While financially responsible, she would be driven by experiences, have wide-ranging interests, yet her family would be first in her life. What else that meant about her, I wasn't certain; I would have to learn more about her.

When I started dating again, I tried a different approach: I became a gentleman, mostly, and much more selective. Although I widened my search, I hardly dated at all. No more going out just to go out; I only asked women who interested me and seemed to have the potential for a long-term relationship.

Talking
Thank you for having dinner
and the pleasant conversation.
Perhaps you would consider
a more private invitation.

Let's go back to my apartment,
where we can have another drink,
and listen to music for entertainment.
What do you think?

   I know you think you're sexy.
   I know you think you're hot.
   But if you think I'm easy,
   well, easy I'm not.

I didn't mean any disrespect
and that's not what I thought,
but after dinner what did you expect,
more drinks and dancing, then what?

Perhaps we might find a diner,
where we could talk over coffee
so I could get to know you better
and you could learn more about me?

EMERGING FLOWERS IN WRANGELL-ST. ELIAS NATIONAL PARK

YELLOWSTONE RIVER AND LOWER FALLS, YELLOWSTONE NATIONAL PARK, WYOMING

CHAPTER 2: *Infatuation*

What if not love,
but only a delirium
of passion carried
by enthusiasm
until it collapses,
momentum spent?

EXHILARATION

The tail end of March 2013 brought snowstorms to the Appalachian Trail. The short days and snow followed by mud and slippery trails forced hikers to proceed slowly.

I was becoming a better and stronger hiker. Usually I kept up with the younger hikers on flatter terrain and going downhill, but fell behind going uphill. At 61, when I stepped on the gas, there came a short-lived burst of energy before resuming my usual slow uphill pace.

Rocky terrain, however, seemed to be my forte. When young, I had worked in a factory with raised tracks of metal rollers along which heavy items moved. For safety, we were supposed to walk around these tracks. Of course, we ignored this rule, cutting across the rollers to save time and steps. One quickly became sure-footed or injured by falling onto those hard iron tracks. Because of this training, I sped across the rocks, never falling.

My facility with rocks was fortuitous. Besides the natural distribution of rocks and stone along the Trail, sections of the AT were constructed by throwing every available rock onto the Trail to control erosion and limit the growth of vegetation. Consequently, at times hiking was like walking on a rocky creek bed except the rocks had not been smoothed by running water but instead remained jagged and sharp. In other places, we struggled across fields of boulders or gingerly crossed rock tables that tilted toward steep slopes and cliffs.

Moisture, however, was my nemesis. Ice, mud, wet flat rocks, streams, and damp stiles—triangular ladders to climb over fences and barbed wire— all brought me down, alarming my companions. Most of the time, my back- pack cushioned the fall. Once I fell onto a large rock, turning a butt cheek into one big bruise. I both heard and felt rock hitting bone. I limped for days and slept on my other side.

The only truly dangerous fall occurred at a jump-off point north of Cheoh Bald after Franklin, North Carolina. The jump-off, I assume, was named as a place where hang gliders (or unfortunate lovers?) leapt. It was a relatively flat rock clear of rubble and other debris. I arrived after a rain, slipped on the wet rock, and fell onto my backpack. The backpack kept me from sliding or rolling. Standing up, I fell again, this time closer to the edge. I shouted, "God!"

Whose Name?

I stood on a precipice and did not fall
then slipped and fell, rose and fell again.
For my companions, I did not yell.
Whose name did I call?

April 2013 was beautiful on the Appalachian Trail. The worst snow-storms were over. Without the cover of snow and ice, easy sections of the Trail appeared. The nights were cold, down into the 20s and 30s, excellent sleeping weather, and the daytime temperatures were ideal for hiking.

MOMENTS ALONG A TRAIL

Looking at pictures I took, I am amazed at how well the eye can pierce through dense trees and brush in a way that the camera cannot.

Although there was less rain that year, water was readily available from the many springs that would dry up during future months. Trees and bushes hadn't filled out yet, leaving open views that soon would be hidden. Looking at pictures I took, I am amazed at how well the eye can pierce through dense trees and brush in a way that the camera cannot. Wildlife was slowly moving uphill as temperatures rose and plants emerged. Unlike the festival atmosphere at Springer, the trails here were uncrowded. Only the long-hikers remained.

VIEW FROM CHEOH BALD NEAR FRANKLIN, NORTH CAROLINA

In the early days, hiking the Appalachian Trail was delightful: the air was cool, clean, and crisp; every mountain, an accomplishment; every vista, amazing; every town, a cornucopia of welcomed luxuries; and every person, fascinating.

Mountains started and ended easily enough but each ascent revealed a unique character and on the other side, the descent would be a completely different experience. Some mountains climbed straight up or down on eroded paths. Others ascended or descended back and forth across rocky switchbacks, sometimes almost circling a mountain before turning back. Some paths sloped so steeply that steps had been constructed using logs, rock, and dirt or cut into stone. These steps functioned like small dams creating slippery lakes behind and miniature waterfalls following a rain. In a few places, water had washed away the fill behind the wood, turning the steps into hurdles over which to clamber, carefully selecting a steady spot to step among the rubble left behind. A few spots required actual climbing, a welcome opportunity to use the muscles in my arms and chest, because I was rapidly losing upper body strength.

Several paths led along cliffs. Shenandoah had two long climbs on narrow, rocky paths beside cliffs providing beautiful views, one up along the Franklin Cliffs and one down to Luray, Virginia. Most mountains topped and then descended, but others merged into ridgelines. Somewhere, possibly near Greenville, North Carolina, one twisted, exposed ridgeline required climbing up and down large blocks placed as huge steps. I marveled at the construction and was puzzled by its accomplishment on such a narrow path. A young lady with short legs, upon confronting each set of blocks, declared, "You must be kidding." She hiked with me that day because, although she left early and arrived late, she couldn't keep up with her friends. Then she got sick and left the Trail a few days later. Much of central and northern Pennsylvania consisted of long ridgelines covered with beds of sharp rocks, fields of boulders, edges of shale, and slabs tilted like dominoes that had fallen against one another. There was a Trail saying that Pennsylvania was where boots go to die. One boot did die and the other was severely wounded.

When I approached a town, I looked forward to picking up a package from my daughters, to see what special treat they had included this time and to reading their notes.

For the first 500 miles of my journey, from Springer into southern Virginia, the towns were far apart with few stores and restaurants near the Trail. At Muskrat Shelter on a cold snowy night, a young man began talking about Franklin, North Carolina, the nearest town, in a way that reminded me of a song from *The Music Man*. He started, "They've got things in Franklin, things like hot water from taps in walls." Quickly others joined in, each of us adding something we missed, especially foods we craved.

Each trekker seemed to crave a different food. Oddly, while others dreamed of steaks, pizzas, fresh fruits and vegetables, or cold beer, I developed a craving for yogurt to calm my stomach, which was having a hard time adjusting to the volume and types of foods I was eating. Apart from fruit, vegetables, and oatmeal, healthy foods stuck in my throat. Instead, my intake consisted of high-fat, high-carb, low-fiber foods, too many snacks, candy, and baked goods that I usually avoided on top of mounds of fatty meats, peanut butter, and nuts.

When I approached a town, I looked forward to picking up a package from my daughters, to see what special treat they had included this time and to reading their notes. Also, I could mail home letters containing my poems, and my cell phone and backup charger could be recharged so I could call my daughters and my mother from the Trail.

When I arrived at a town, no matter how small or how sparse the facilities, I was grateful for the opportunity to shower, to do laundry, purchase supplies, eat hot food cooked and brought to me by other people, and then to sleep on a bed or bunk with a mattress of sorts in a heated room with a roof overhead and indoor plumbing conveniently nearby. Even the most Spartan accommodations felt luxurious. Then, to leave town clean and rested, wearing fresh, good-smelling clothes, carrying a pack full of foods I craved and an unjustifiably way-too-heavy special treat for the first night out, well, that was heavenly.

Hikers were interesting in their own ways. Day-hikers and campers had information about the path ahead and stories to share about their section of the Trail. In Tennessee, I wished for a grilled-cheese sandwich to go with a packet of instant tomato soup that my daughters had sent. A young Tennessean said, "I can make that happen." He pulled out some bread and cheese and made me a grilled-cheese sandwich. While I waited, his parents explained that the shelters had been encased in chain-link fences, which had to be taken down. Because some campers fed bears through the fences, the bears began to frequent the shelters, presenting a danger to other hikers. They also told me about a young man who had recently been mauled by a bear when he ran out of the hot dogs that he was stupidly feeding the bear.

I never could tell the difference between an elaboration and a fabrication of a trail story. There were many tall tales. Yet, many improbable events happen on a long hike, thus there always is a possibility that an unlikely sounding story might be true, if only approximately so.

Along the Blue Ridge Parkway, a group watching the hawk migration asked me to sit with them for a while. They gave me drinks and snacks then told me the "inside" story of murders on the Trail years before. They said the murderer never made it to trial, but instead died in jail. In Duncannon, Pennsylvania, an old-timer entertained me with story after story about famous hikers, including one story supposedly about Earl Shaffer, the first through-hiker, who walked into a camp unannounced and sat quietly listening as people told stories about him.

South of the James River, a volunteer told me the story behind the Foot Bridge. On most bridges, hikers walk on the narrow, raised borders next to the guardrails, unnervingly close to fast-moving vehicles. However, hikers cross the James River on a foot bridge, curiously named the Foot Bridge. William and Laurel Foot had convinced the owner of the now-unused railroad bridge to donate the piers to the Appalachian Conservancy, which then obtained grants to construct a bridge for the hikers to cross the wide river safely. The volunteer said he had worked with William Foot at one time and they became lasting friends when the Foots helped him plan his expedition biking coast-to-coast across the United States on the American Discovery Trail, which William and Laurel had been the first people to complete. To me, the James River area is one of the most beautiful sections of the Trail. It has nice views on the way in, followed by a river walk in the shade of cliffs, and then a nice climb out along a cascading stream.

In almost every sector of the Trail, a local would claim that their portion of the Trail was the hardest part. They were both right and wrong; every section of the Trail was the hardest for some hiker, but not necessarily for every hiker.

Fellow trekkers had information to share. They had new stories or jokes and updates about the other trekkers. Of all things, in 2014, I spent a night at Rock Spring Hut in Shenandoah with a young man hiking south to complete the balance of his trek from the prior year. He had hiked with one of my young friends, Photo Bomber, who had left the Trail to take an internship. Photo Bomber had great speed and stamina. One day, he hiked more than 30 miles to catch up to us at Overmountain Shelter, a large red barn. At summer's end, Bomber hiked south, completing the Trail in the cold and snow of late December, something he does not recommend to anyone.

Humor was greatly appreciated on the Trail, amusing if only for the attempt. Once atop a mountain, suddenly I sneezed explosively. From far down below came a voice, "God bless you." We met at a hostel later. When I told the story, he exclaimed, "That was me!" I got quite a few laughs with that simple story.

Some hikers would read imaginary entries from a trail register at a shelter. "Congratulations, you have won $100,000 for being the 100,000th hiker to stay at this shelter." Or, "Wanted: smelly, dirty, hungry, desperate men willing to work for food, shower, and bed." We all volunteered. Some trekkers wrote amusing comments in the trail registers. One hiker wrote, "It was a good day: the Trail didn't try to kill me."

Each trekker had a tip or advice to share, from my asking or watching what gear they used to enquiring about what they did in certain situations. These were natural starting points for conversation, for example, "How is that filter working for you?" or at camp, "What are you eating tonight?"

One of the biggest decisions and a frequent topic of discussion was when to send your heavy winter gear home. Switch to your warm-weather gear too early and you risked being caught in a late-spring snowstorm or by a cold front with heavy, deadly cold rain. In April 2014, several through-hikers racing to Katahdin had made that mistake and were rushing to reach a town before a cold front moved in.

There was a spirit of camaraderie among the trekkers. We had been bumping into each other for a few weeks on the Trail, in shelters and campsites. It was hard to learn the names of the young men, because there were so many of them and our appearances continued to change as our hair and beards grew. Yet, we grew to recognize each other from a distance, by our general appearance and gear, and by the way we moved. I recognized one young man by his distinctive gait. He asked, "What does that mean?" He knew the word but was concerned that he might appear odd. I explained, "We all have our own way of walking," to which he agreed, adding he hadn't thought about that.

After the snowstorm at Muskrat, four of us went for dinner in Franklin, North Carolina. It was one of the most delightful social evenings of my life, happy to be warm, in a small-town Italian restaurant, eating town foods—

baskets of Italian bread, salads, and pastas—drinking beer, talking, joking, and laughing. We talked about our lives and families, and about the Trail, taking turns at swapping stories. At one point during dinner, I thought to myself, *It doesn't get any better than this.*

After the first few weeks, trekking had become delightful. Once my feet and legs were ready, I had lost a few pounds, and I'd lightened my pack, bit by bit, discarding unused items, my trek became a wonderful, grand adventure. No matter how steep or treacherous, the Trail seemed easy; the vistas, magnificent; the towns, pleasing; the hikers and everything else, perfect. I felt born to the Trail. Ordinarily I never sing, but on those glorious days, I sang loudly.

ENCHANTMENT

In 2010, I was finally in a relationship that seemed to be working. We had started suddenly; like thunder and lightning, we were electric. One of the jokes about online dating was the instant relationship: take one man, add one woman, shake and there it is: a relationship. We were like that; one moment we were apart and then we were fused together, as quickly as that.

For the purpose of this book, I felt the need to give my lady friend a trail name. Because our relationship was a turning point in my life, I thought of Hecate Trivia, the ancient goddess of crossroads. However, the name "He-ca-te" carries connotations of magic and witchcraft, whereas Trivia would sound like an insult to a modern ear even though Tri-via literally means three way(s). Research revealed a similar name, Triveni Sangam, from Sanskrit and Hindi, which refers to the meeting place of three (sacred) rivers. I chose Triveni (tree-vain-e) to represent the confluence of my personal life with my newfound loves of hiking and writing.

She approached me first, because she had owned a basset hound that resembled our Otis. Triveni was a beautiful, blue-eyed, blond Scandinavian, seven years younger. We had dinner and began dating.

Otis took to her right away. She knew the right spots to scratch. Her dogs accepted me. My daughters and family liked her. Triveni's family thought I was "so normal," which gave me pause, but thought it best not to explore this statement more closely lest my own past be inspected. We had many things in common. We had both grown up in western Pennsylvania and been to many of the same places nearby. Our fathers had even died and been buried on the same days.

Yet, we were a contrast. While I loved to learn, it being my favorite thing, I was adequate but not especially athletic. I just liked, not loved, to play sports and so was never quite dedicated enough to earn a spot on a competitive team. My talents were decidedly more academic. An athletic scholarship had never been a dream of mine, whereas she was accomplished athletically as well as academically. She had been skiing, hiking, and camping her entire life. She had climbed, rappelled, and even gone scuba diving. I never thought to attempt such things.

Everything fell into place easily for Triveni and me. I have known couples who claimed it happened for them that way. Now it seemed it was happening for us. Everything seemed to be aligning. We were both ready for a relationship and it seemed we had finally found someone compatible who was sane, normal, responsible, and unencumbered by their past, substance abuse, illness, debt, or interfering responsibilities.

However, Triveni did have a commitment that required her to be on the West Coast for part of the summer. She asked me to help drive her four-wheel drive vehicle out there. I had never driven cross-country before or been to the western national parks, whereas she had been there many times. Triveni planned our route and schedule, picking places for us to visit. We camped and day-hiked along the way.

BEAR PREP

I had never really hiked or ever camped before meeting Triveni. Apart from modest attempts at a paternal rite in our suburban backyard where I would encamp with young children eager for a modest adventure replete with stories and snacks, then spend a restful night alone as children, quickly bored once stories ended and snacks ran out, would one-by-one abandon me, initially lured indoors by the plumbing, and then stay, seduced by the easy luxury of cozy couches, movies, copious snacks, and warm familiar bedding. No, I had never really camped before Triveni.

Thankfully, Triveni knew what she was doing during our first summer camping, because I was naive and unprepared. In one of my less-than-brilliant schemes, to protect us against any bear that dared to violate our tent, I took a long fireplace lighter to bed with me to set the offending bear on fire. As if I really might have the presence of mind to find a lighter during a bear attack. Not to mention that I sometimes struggled to light those things back home under more normal circumstances, without the additional stress of our diaphanous tent being shredded around us. I had also not considered the consequences of setting a bear on fire in our suddenly over-crowded, flammable tent, incinerating it and us along with it. Nor had I thought about sending a frightened, angry bear fleeing through a dry park, shedding sparks and bits of burning fur at the peak of the summer camping season. A rather dumb idea, I admit.

Happily for us, the bears, campers, and campgrounds, we never did encounter a bear in our tent or out of our tent. Nowadays, I try not to take offense when I receive packs of those lighters as gifts, reminders of my poorly thought-out security.

In my defense, two people, one while sleeping, died from bear attacks later that year near where we had stopped for a leisurely lunch one day. The next summer, we purchased matching canisters of bear spray.

During our ten-day, 2,700 mile trip to the coast in 2010, the beauty of the American West awakened an appreciation of nature that had lain dormant in me for a long time. Was it nature's beauty alone that affected me? Or, was it from sharing the experience with someone I felt close to? Perhaps the exertion of day-hiking, which combined with being enveloped by nature, heightened my senses. Regardless of the reasons, I was enthralled with the beauty of the American West.

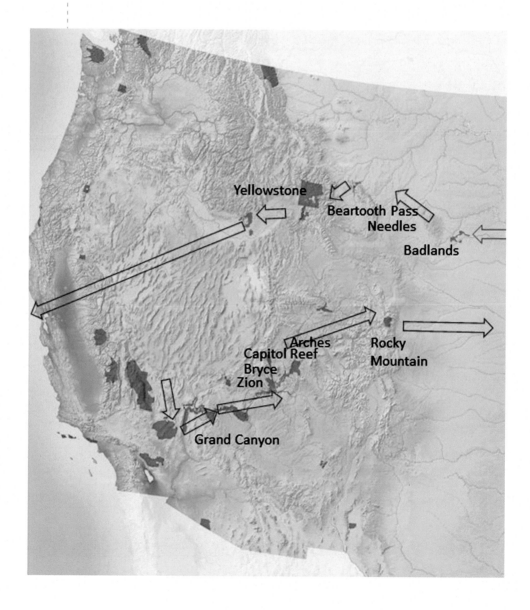

When I'm hiking, I say that I left my pride in the parking lot.

We stopped first at the Badlands National Park in South Dakota. Never had I imagined such a landscape of sculptured sandstone rising in sharp knife edges and plunging into deep-cut canyons. The movies did not compare to reality.

In the Badlands, I had my first exposure to "hiking" as opposed to walking. The Notch Trail is 1.5 miles roundtrip. The National Park Service cautions those who are afraid of heights not to attempt this trail.

The first quarter mile of the Notch Trail leads to a ladder made by thick, three-foot- long logs hung between two steel cables. Once up the ladder, we took a terrifying walk on a narrow, tilted path along a cliff until we reached about a 10-foot-high rock outcrop blocking our way. A sign pointed to the right, cautioning us not to skirt the outcrop by crossing the steep slope to the left but to proceed to the right where we needed to climb up and over the rock before proceeding to a spectacular view. It was perhaps 75 to 100 feet down to the rocks below.

This was too much risk for me on my first exposure to hiking; I turned back. Triveni scurried across the slopes like a mountain goat, while I crawled along the edge. When I'm hiking, I say that I left my pride in the parking lot. My primary objective is to return unharmed.

From the Badlands we went to Custer State Park in South Dakota, where we drove the Needles Highway. I'm not sure whether the Needles Highway deserves to be named for the tall, needle-like spines of rock, one with a cutout resembling the eye of a needle, or more because the drive was like threading a needle along a narrow road with steep, long drop offs to one side. Somehow I felt safer in the car rather than hiking in the Badlands until we drove past a family standing next to the road,

THE LADDER ON THE NOTCH TRAIL IN THE BADLANDS NATIONAL PARK, SOUTH DAKOTA

BEARTOOTH PASS,
MONTANA

their car caught by a tree 30 feet below. They looked to be unharmed, although a young man seemed distraught. I wondered, *Had he been driving?* The Needles Highway was not a place where the driver could safely admire the view. I drove, Triveni admitted to closing her eyes, and neither of us got a good look at the scenery.

In order to approach Yellowstone National Park from the east, we drove sharp switchbacks over Beartooth Pass. Imagine climbing up the side of the mountain with switchbacks like stairs running back-and-forth between landings where you can look up and down the valley, at other mountains this way or that, and down to watch other vehicles following you. The switchbacks are sharp; the pass is not a place for trailers. At the top we drove between snowbanks still towering over our car in mid-June.

The richness of Yellowstone amazed me: numerous hot springs, herds of elk and buffalo, an occasional solitary moose, and countless spectacular vistas and views. *How long had it taken to make the steaming salt steps and plateaus?* The highlight of our drive to the West Coast was standing on a cliff overlooking the Yellowstone River and Lower Falls. I stood among rocks, brush, and fallen branches above a steep drop off. Before me, to the left and right, like motionless guards, stood solid, clean rock cliffs between and beneath which the Yellowstone River wildly leapt over the Lower Falls, then galloped onward in a blue-and-white tumult. It reminded me of a scene from a movie I had watched many times with my daughters when Cinderella runs down the palace steps with her blue dress and white petticoats flowing with her. The scene before me was more perfect than any picture or movie. I was childlike in awe.

Somewhere, I had lost the sense of wonder with which we are born. Everything, it seemed, had become commonplace to me. Had I been too busy making a living? Had I become too smart, too sophisticated? Not that the world had given up trying to impress me. The universe held one trick in reserve, for when I became a father, I had seen the world renewed through my children's eyes. Will the world be reborn again when I become a grandfather?

Wondrous Eyes
When I was a young boy,
before I became so very wise,
everything was for me to enjoy
and I saw the world through wondrous eyes.
Every sight was astonishing
and often bewildering;
each sensation, surprising;
pain overwhelmingly so
and pleasure, ever so sensuous,
like ice cream or chocolate savored,
drawing a luxurious blanket
over my body in my youth.

But in a slow, unrelenting transition,
like a photograph left in the sun,
colors weakened and shapes blurred
until new formations emerged.
I viewed the world through serious eyes:

THE SALT STEPS
AND PLATEAU OF
THE MAIN TERRACE,
YELLOWSTONE
NATIONAL PARK

a bridge became a crossing,
a skyscraper, a building;
the sun, moon, and stars at night,
good light, weak light, and meager light;
no longer astonishing,
no longer surprising,
a world made magicless;
and I, jaded in my youth.

The world might break through:
the sun or moon large on the horizon,
or another spectacular view,
forcing my oblivious eyes
to open in reflex;
or by an intense impression:
a cold beer in summer,
a delicate dish at dinner,
and the marvelous discovery of sex;
or with subversive subtlety:

a song and a singer,
a woman stunningly beautiful
and I momentarily youthful.

When I became a father,
I recognized the wonder
in my daughter's curious eyes,
as when holding her
before a three-sided mirror,
her seeing our numerous reflections,
looking back and forth from the mirror
to me holding her,
cautiously pressing her fingers against the mirror,
until suddenly looking at herself aware.
I don't know how long we stood there engaged,
her with the mirror and I with her,
but too soon my children aged
and were no longer young.

Standing before this great expanse,
I feel born again, perhaps my last chance
to see the world through wondrous eyes.
Although I can still carry supplies
up and down a mountain,
I can feel myself aging.
I'm slowing down.
And my friends keep dying.

If a courteous young man
were to ask my sage advice,
I would say: "Live life urgently.
Do all you want to do while you can,
be a mindful witness
to the ever-changing sky and restless seas,
to aged mountains motionless,
to emerald valleys and forests,
to fertile rivers and prairies,
to the brazen, naked beauty
of the desert and great dry West
and regardless of the weather
to give thanks for every blessed day,
for the gracious gift that is water,

for teeming life resilient,
a happy woman singing,
the laughter of children playing,
a trusted friend's true loyalty
and to see the world through an artist's eyes."

When Triveni and I arrived at the coast, I boarded a plane to fly home while she stayed in San Francisco to complete her summer commitment. To every romance, there is a period of enchantment, a thrilling time when lovers discard caution and take risks. Our chemistry was strong and our fevers, hot. We excited one another. We were the most interesting people in the world to each other.

In anticipation of being apart, Triveni and my relationship had intensified during the drive. Was it the afterglow from our journey through the West? Or, was this only the initial delight of another promising relationship, rekindled by our time and drive together? Once again it became a sweet, deep infatuation. We spoke of how strongly we had bonded and how much we would miss each other. We vowed to keep in touch and be loyal to each other. We were impatient to meet again.

In the Morning
I couldn't sleep thinking about you, darling.
Nothing I did could quiet this yearning.
I hoped we might meet in the morning.

I wandered from room to room,
trying every couch, bed, and chair,
but could not rest anywhere.

Have you ever known a night so long;
a morning to be so distant;
a time, so empty and quiet?

Have you been neither asleep nor awake;
trapped in a dream unending;
lost in a fog not breaking?

What is this thirst, I cannot quench;
this hunger, I cannot quell;
this craving that so compels?

Without your presence,
my life remains suspended;
every moment wasted.

Although the day broke clear and bright,
we did not meet in the morning
and not that day or evening.

Have you ever known desire so deep,
it robs you of sleep?
When, oh when, will we meet?

There comes a magical night, not necessarily the first night of making love, but a glorious night of union: emotionally, physically, and spiritually intimate.

Words at Night
Words slip past a sleepy censor
bearing promises sweet and tender.

Thoughts unspoken find expression,
passion uncovered, not yet done.

We turn to kiss, bodies align,
wanting this union of yours and mine.

We touch and tease, laugh and confide
in love's final pleasure.

Can king or queen claim anything
to rival love's private treasure?

⁂

There would follow a period of obsession, more than physical, which was addictive in its intensity. Is it any wonder that some people move from one relationship to another hoping to recapture this excitement?

Triveni and I were like young lovers and old lovers. We held hands while we walked. We kissed in public. There was a natural intimate way in how we spoke with and looked at each other. We exchanged glances that said, "I know what you're thinking." When we walked around towns, people assumed we were married.

HIKING OUT FROM MUSKRAT SHELTER, NORTH CAROLINA

CHAPTER 3: *Evaluation*

Or just a game,
like careless children pretending,
a game each too kind to end,
or still playing
to avoid blame for ending
a game gone errant?

MOTIVATION

At some point on the Appalachian Trail in both 2013 and 2014, the magic began to wear off. Inconveniences began to annoy me. There was a trail phrase, the "pointless-up-and-down," referring to instances when we were sent up and down a mountain when there was an easier route around the mountain. In the Grayson Highlands, Virginia, the Trail led out and onto a large pile of rocks offering a better view of the area. On the way back, I was surprised to see trekkers about 50 yards to my right following the same path to the rocks. We waved forlornly to each other. It seemed as if the Trail was designed to cover every mountain and rock between Georgia and Maine.

Sometimes the trail crossed back and forth across a stretch of rock before moving forward. South of Port Clinton, Pennsylvania, the Trail led across boulders, then turned back across the boulders again before shooting straight down the steepest, slipperiest, longest slope thus far right into the railroad yard outside of town. My friend Cruise said she fell going down that slope in rain the year before. It seemed cruel to lead us over the same boulder field again.

Almost every mountain led to a view, so many vistas that they became less exhilarating by their repetition. Once the trees leaves came out to hide the views, I began to appreciate the vistas more because they were infrequent.

Eventually, I became critical, quickly moving on because a view wasn't as astounding as the last. I began to notice deficiencies in the offerings of each small mountain town. Some trekkers began to annoy me, and I sensed I began to annoy some others.

VIEW IN
SHENANDOAH
NATIONAL PARK,
VIRGINIA

I reminded myself that this endeavor was entirely voluntary. I could stop at any point, but still got up every morning, hiked all day, camped at night, and then got up to do it all over again. I did my miles, filled the days, passed the time, but began to feel that I needed a reason to continue. "Why are you hiking?" I asked other trekkers.

Trekkers

Have you ever thought to join with trekkers,
to consider leaving your sanctuary,
to making plans and collecting the right
gear, only to pause, telling yourself "someday,"
knowing "never" will you ever keep
that appointment, with perhaps a thousand
reasons not to go? If you stay
at home as millions do, feel no disgrace:
there are valid reasons not to clamber
about distant mountains, things
do go wrong. Perhaps though the long absence
itself prevents most journeys.
Your interests, duties, and honor lie elsewhere.

Yet each year about three thousand hikers
leave all that is dear behind and boldly
travel to far-away remote sites
to start up a mountain to walk a long way
for many months. They take this risky leap

in hope, neither compelled nor requested,
unless by a companion. They
know only one in five will win the race—
six months—against the approaching winter
and still they come out every spring.
Perhaps one in eight will finish the balance
of their trek another year. Thus one in three
might complete the challenge, a rare
accomplishment to little recognition
except from a few good friends and family.

Makes you wonder: what drives these dreamers,
doesn't it? Are they all fools or just crazy?
Of all that I heard, my favorite
reason is the celebratory, "hooray,"
having postponed, for a while, that last sleep.
Then there are those who feel obligated,
to complete, as best they may,
a walking epitaph taking the place
of a loved one. As for any hiker:
pure love of hiking and camping,
a pilgrimage to purify one's conscience,
or an escape from responsibility,
perhaps simply that it is there,
to prove one's mettle as a true outdoorsman,
or to complete one thing in life triumphantly.

And for the younger hiker,
perhaps a fantasy; or seeking
to test the limits of one's youthful endurance;
feeling lost to find one's true identity;
or courageously to dare;
a final fling, a last harmless indiscretion
before assuming a life of respectability.

As to the older hiker,
perhaps a lifelong dream; or mourning
over a spouse, marriage, or child; a last indulgence;
a final "hurrah"; or just something for me,
after a lifetime of service, square
things a bit, you know; or to climb a mountain,
stand there unbowed, and stare down eternity.

On April 27, 2014, I started from Dick's Dome Shelter, milepost 979, hoping to reach the Blackburn Center, milepost 1005, and set a personal record, my first 26-mile day.

Perhaps the best thing to bring on the Trail was a good, clear reason to sustain you through to Katahdin in Maine.

COMMEMORATIVE HIKERS

Some trekkers hiked in memory of a loved one: in the Smokies, a Korean woman honoring her husband's dream; in Pennsylvania, a young man who carried his hiker-mother's ashes; also in Pennsylvania, seven men coming out for a week at a time, bringing along the ashes of a friend; and a man near my age who carried his brother's ashes to Katahdin. Others hiked in celebration of having escaped life-threatening illnesses. A young man told of his bout with cancer; a middle-aged man, about heart disease and his operations—he never expected to be able to fulfill his lifelong dream to hike the Appalachian Trail; and an old man his treatments for cancer, now in remission, for who knew how long. *What better way to celebrate a reprieve than to immerse one's self in nature?*

Trekkers encountered the mental challenge at different points; I called this "a moment of reality." There was no telling when the utter insanity of trekking tested your will. What was difficult for one may not be difficult for another. Moreover, this mental challenge happens not once, but repeatedly and differently—that, I think, is the difference between hiking and trekking. I can endure almost anything for a week, but week after week there came a new challenge. At first, the physical challenges dominated, then emotional issues emerged, loneliness and homesickness, until a person begins to doubt the necessity of continuing. *Why am I doing this? Is this worth it? What do I have to prove?* And then all of these would appear, in varying amounts, at any moment, a mixture of the physical, emotional, and mental.

Trekkers talked about losing their appetite from the exertion of hiking long distances day after day, until at some point a "Great Hunger" set in, when everyone wanted to eat all they could, all of the time.

There is an old survivalist saying, called the Rule of Threes: you can survive without air for three minutes, without shelter for three hours, without water for three days, and without food for three weeks. For the first few weeks, I ate a bit more than usual, but not commensurate with the increase in my daily activity. I simply wasn't any hungrier. Meanwhile, my body was consuming its reserves. Eventually, my body rebelled, demanding to be fed. More than any other single thing, I think that moment separates a long hike from a trek, the moment when your body finally shouts, "Hey! I need to be fed."

On the hardest days, I struggled into camp with everything aching, not a hurting, painful ache, more like a headache except not one headache but a hundred as every muscle and joint complained. I would lie down flat on my back, try to stretch out my legs, and wait while slowly my legs and back would straighten as my knees and spine lowered to the ground pulled by gravity as I relaxed. I would stay like that, enjoying the support from under me, imagining myself being held by the earth, sometimes falling asleep. I slept so deeply, soundly, and still that others would check to see if I was alive. If not disturbed, I slept until I felt the call of nature, then stumbled into the woods, where I released a foul-smelling fluid, after which I was fine. My system could process toxins only so quickly, drinking more water helped—I did and do drink lots of water. My body just needed the time.

The hardest part of the Trail for me was in Virginia, a 9-mile section of the Roller Coaster ending at Bear's Den Hostel. The Roller Coaster takes hikers straight up and down across 10 peaks in 13 miles and that day, across swollen streams as well. The total elevation gain was about 4,000 feet give or take a few hundred, which was not an unusual amount. However, the constant up and down taxed my endurance.

On April 27, 2014, I started from Dick's Dome Shelter, milepost 979, hoping to reach the Blackburn Center, milepost 1005, and set a personal record, my first 26-mile day. Day hikers warned me about an approaching cold front bringing heavy rain. Younger hikers ran by me, rushing to reach Blackburn before the storm. I was slowing down as I approached Bear's Den Hostel and would need another four hours to reach Blackburn. So, I decided to stop around 3 p.m. at Bear's Den, knowing I could get a spot inside. It was a respectable 18-mile day. The storm proved to be dangerous; some hikers wearing summer gear arrived at Bear's Den bordering on hypothermia.

Yet, it wasn't the difficulty or a problem that created a crisis. Rather the challenges of snow; rain; rough terrain; and long, hard days all gave meaning to a trek and rallied our spirits. We would not allow ourselves to be defeated by the current challenge.

BRYANT RIDGE
SHELTER, VIRGINIA:
A NICE SHELTER
WITH A PORCH, A
VENTILATED SECOND
STORY, AND SET
ON HIGH GROUND
ABOVE A CREEK
PROVIDING WATER.

Many trekkers actually weakened during the absence of difficulties. When the weather was good, the Trail was easy, and water was plentiful, the monotony of trekking proved to be the greatest challenge. It might happen in a town when a trekker seduced by luxury finally declared, "I've had enough. I'm going home."

A lot of hikers dropped off in Virginia. It was a long state, over 500 miles, a quarter of the entire Appalachian Trail. In 2013, when we arrived at southern Virginia, the mountains had greened out. We were hiking in a green tunnel, with long distances between inspiring vistas. Some say the Trail gets easier when you enter Virginia. If so, we hiked faster and longer when it was less challenging and thus the effort didn't feel any easier at the end of the day. We'd been on the Trail for two months—that's a long time and for many, that was long enough.

An unexpected setback could be discouraging. In 2013, the first such challenge came in the form of a disease. Norovirus, the scourge of cruise ships, is a nasty illness. Hikers were waking up vomiting or defecating, ruining their gear or soiling shelters. A friend with connections to the Appalachian Conservancy said more than half of hikers were estimated to be infected with the norovirus at that time. I never caught the norovirus, because I had stayed in Hot Springs, Virginia, while others were catching it. Outside Hot Springs, signs warned hikers to avoid the shelters and privies, wash their hands frequently, and never share food with anyone.

It's hard to overstate the importance of hygiene on the Trail. It's never fun to be sick anywhere, but especially not in a shelter miles from the nearest town. Chances are, you probably will get sick at some point; the purpose of hygiene is to prevent avoidable illnesses. An Alaska outdoorsman once reminded us that we were hiking in someone else's bathroom. Wherever we were, some creature had been there before us. He wanted us to be careful, not to make us paranoid, but his words and advice resonated with me.

Shelters and privies were the only conveniences on the Trail. Yet, staying in a shelter or using a privy risked exposure to whatever disease was going around at the time. Norovirus forced everyone away from the shelters and privies and out into the woods instead.

At best, shelters and privies were a mixed blessing. Staying in a shelter accelerated setup at night and tear-down in the morning. Most shelters were three-sided, well-constructed, single-story shacks sleeping between four and eight, sometimes more. Most had a fire pit and a picnic table to cook and eat on. Keep in mind that every board, nail, block, post, and beam and every bag of cement had to be carried or ferried along the Trail. That anything stood in some locations was a testimonial to the perseverance of the hiking clubs supporting the Trail.

However, shelters harbored mice and other critters. Mice would chew holes to get at food left in pockets and packs. One night, chipmunks busily slipped dozens of acorns into my backpack hanging on a peg. Another night, my head lay near the entry and exit point for mice. I abandoned that shelter to sleep on a picnic table. I never did get used to mice bouncing across my sleeping pad. Once I rolled over, thereby trapping a mouse under the edge of it. The critter's frantic scratching and struggling wakened me. I rolled over to the other side in order to free him and then went back to sleep.

Shelters could be noisy, what with traffic, conversation, cooking, snoring, and other sleep sounds. We were all eating unhealthy, high-calorie foods, challenging our digestive systems, eating too much candy and peanut butter. At Deep Gap Shelter, milepost 63, I was caught in a childhood cartoon of men snoring in a bunkhouse. A symphony performed that night: a deep snorer, a high-pitched snorer, a whistler, a cougher, a wheezer, a mutterer, and occasional tweets, horns, and tubas, all to the rat-a-tat-tat of scurrying mice.

The best part of a shelter was that it offered a roof over my head on a rainy night. During torrential rains in 2013, 22 hikers crammed into a shelter built for 6 that was south of Marion, Virginia. In the morning, streams

were impassible. Friends arriving in Marion showed me a picture of a bridge above a once-gentle stream. It was a particularly picturesque scene—I had stopped to take a photo there two days before. But what I saw now was that the bridge had been overrun by waves of cascading water, far too dangerous for anyone to attempt crossing.

A heavy rain doesn't gently flow down a mountainside; it violently crashes into everything in its way.

When the wind was strong, more experienced hikers skipped the shelters, choosing instead to stay in their tents, which provided better protection from the wind. A strong wind rips right through an unshielded sleeping bag in an open shelter, spiriting away warmth. I used an emergency reflective blanket to block the wind as much as for the added heat. However, the emergency blanket trapped moisture. In the morning, the outside of my sleeping bag would be covered in a heavy dew that needed to dry before being packed away. Fortunately, it resisted absorbing moisture.

By the way, don't ever set up your tent next to a fallen log. Fallen logs make great toilet seats.

Privies were a convenience. However, they also attracted wildlife. A porcupine had taken up residence under the privy at Clark Ferry Shelter, milepost 1141. Good luck to anyone who disturbed him! I could see the grating surrounding the base of the privy had been pulled back to gain access, but didn't check if he was at home. Spiders loved the dark, damp privies. One acquaintance was bitten on his bum by a brown recluse spider, requiring medical attention and ongoing medication. Now, I always check for webs and run a stick around inside to see if I stir anything up before taking a seat. It was a long way from the halls of academia and former castles.

Most privies were enclosed. Oddly, a few had no roof and one had no roof or walls, just a seat on a platform set in the woods, and situated visibly near the side trail approaching the shelter. It is a unique experience to sit in an elevated privy with a cold winter wind nipping your behind. Some shelters had no privies at all, just a shovel and a sign pointing the way to a field.

"GOING" IN THE WOODS

There are a couple of tricks for "going" in the woods. Dig a long hole, lest your aim is off, and not too wide, lest you lose your balance. Be mindful of the location of your pants. Don't look for a good place to take a dump, it's already been used. Instead, look for the most difficult, improbable site. There was a cliff in Virginia that some of the locals called "Shit Cliff," which was a little too exposed and risky for me (besides being a gross violation of proper trail etiquette: to leave no trace behind).

By the way, don't ever set up your tent next to a fallen log. Fallen logs make great toilet seats.

Volunteers maintain the shelters, privies, and Trail. Imagine my bewildered amusement to see, reminiscent of a pennant waving in the air over a jousting knight, the business end of a push-broom waving above the cleaner's head as he came up a hill toward me. It was a "cleaner," a volunteer from a hiking club who came out periodically to clean and sanitize the shelters and privies during the norovirus outbreak. It was the only time I have ever met a real "white knight."

Volunteers also removed debris from the Trail. In March and April, they had not yet removed all of the trees that had fallen across the Trail during the winter and spring storms. Thus we had to find a way around, over, or under these trees. Several times, I slithered through mud beneath a trunk, trying not to jostle the tree lest it fall onto me. I would take off my pack, then toss it over or push it ahead of me before carefully sliding on my belly underneath. The first time I wondered, *Should I take off my shirt?* I decided to keep my shirt on and wash it out later. North of Marion, Virginia, after the torrential storm, I found a huge tree blocking the path. To the right was a wide, deep, overflowing stream. The only way around was up a slippery slope of mud, around the tree, then down what was now a mud slide on the other side. The vegetation already had been stripped away by other hikers slipping up and down.

The hiking clubs removed fallen trees and other debris, built and maintained the shelters and privies, created and maintained the trails, and periodically relocated the Trail to control erosion. Constructing switchbacks and rerouting trails is hard, demanding, physical labor. When I crossed paths with club members, I thanked them. The Trail runs through national and state parks, game lands and preserves and close to population centers along the East Coast, and every year, a million or more hikers and campers come out to the Trail along its 2,186-mile length. The Appalachian Trail could not exist without the support of the hiking clubs, all volunteers and all truly "white knights."

For me, the challenge to my resolve came early, in Hot Springs, Virginia, milepost 272, where I said good-bye to my best friends, Slim and Danno. I didn't expect to see them again because they were younger, much faster, and able to do more miles in a day than me. The snow, rain, and mud had slowed the faster hikers to my pace. Now that the weather had broken, it seemed that all of my friends and acquaintances were forging ahead.

It was amazing how quickly and strongly bonds developed between trekkers. Like most men, I had slowly made friends at work, through our spouses or children, or through church and charitable activities. I had not anticipated how quickly I would become attached to my Trail friends, nor how much I relied upon their support and encouragement. It was always an emotional blow to learn that some acquaintance had left the Trail. When someone left, someone we thought was tough, whose presence helped us and inspired us, when they left, it hurt. It felt like a friend had died.

Every day I searched the trail registers for names I knew. Recognizing a name lifted my spirits. Although new registers are put out every year, in 2014, I sometimes found a 2013 book still in place. I eagerly scoured the names from the prior year. It didn't matter whether I knew them well, not even whether I had liked them or they had liked me. We had shared the Trail and it was a joy to know that they had been there. In late 2013 and again in 2014, I stopped at the Appalachian Conservancy Headquarters in Harper's Ferry to look through the names and pictures. I was elated to see that so many I knew had made it that far. I made a list of their names that I keep on my dresser at home. Every once in a while I pick it up and look at those names, associating a face and place with a name so I don't forget them.

Slim and I met on the way to Muskrat Shelter, North Carolina, milepost 79. I was hiking with another trekker and the dog he had rescued in a town along the way. It was snowing so heavily that the vistas we passed were hidden behind a wall of white. The blowing wind reminded me of pictures and films of explorers in the Artic and adventurers climbing Everest. *I'll never do that,* I thought, even though I was comfortably warm hiking in gear tested against the Michigan winter. My rain pants and jacket functioned as wind shells. That night, I would sleep in them to retain the heat.

Slim introduced himself to my hiking companion and me. Slim and I became friends that evening while we endured a miserable night next to each other during the still-blowing snowstorm and temperatures in the teens. Muskrat faced into the wind; the floor was covered with hard-packed snow. A fellow through-hiker helped stretch my tarp across the front to block the deadly wind.

I learned the value of sleeping warm that night; my three-season (spring, summer, and fall) sleeping pad with an insulation value of R-3, wasn't enough for me in that cold and wind. The wind sweeping under the shelter stole warmth from below. My neighbor on my right side—Slim was on my left,

Thankfully, I already had a trail name, or I might have become known as "Snuggles" as a result of that night.

had a better sleeping pad. While asleep, I gradually migrated toward his pad until he nudged me awake with his elbow. Thankfully, I already had a trail name, or I might have become known as "Snuggles" as a result of that night.

Later in Franklin, North Carolina, a soldier recommended a four-season pad, with an insulation value over R-5, like the one he was using and had used in Afghanistan. I knew my body worked to repair and strengthen itself while I was sleeping, but did not know a 200-pound man burns as many as 800 calories overnight. Sleeping cold diverted energy from the necessary repair work toward keeping me warm. Since learning that fact, when camping in the cold, I always have a snack and drink a warm pint of milk before I go to bed. It works; I feel rejuvenated in the morning.

The next day, Slim and I hiked, at times through knee-high snowdrifts, to Deep Gap. The names of some locations recur: Deep Gap, Low Gap, and Sassafras Gap seemed to be the most common. The snow-covered path to Deep Gap was slow going and dangerous because we couldn't tell how far down we were stepping. Slim said he had slipped the day before, tumbled downhill, and stopped safely nestled in the snow beneath a fallen tree. I fell when my backpack shifted because I hadn't secured the straps tightly over my layers of clothing. I directed my fall toward the uphill slope, praying there were no jagged, spear-like wooden branches hidden underneath the snow.

Slim was much more experienced than I; consequently, I benefited more from his companionship than he did from mine. He was a manager adept at interacting with people of all types, whereas I have less patience. He was always cheerful and encouraging and had a way of drawing people into a conversation. He was popular. There was one way I complemented Slim. When his cell phone had no signal, it seemed mine did and vice versa. For much of the Southern mountains, there was limited or no cell phone coverage at all.

When we reached Deep Gap at milepost 83, I thought of the promise I'd made to my daughters. I said to Slim, "This is a dangerous situation." He agreed and called a shuttle driver to give us a lift into Franklin, North Carolina. It seemed every hiker had the same idea; the motels in Franklin were packed. There were rumors of hikers who were not prepared for the bad weather and needed to be rescued from the mountains. There was even word of a young man who was found at midday still in his tent. The rescue crew had used a defibrillator to save him. Later, a waitress in Fontana, North Carolina, said 33 hikers had been taken out of the Smokies and rangers were checking that hikers had gear suitable for the weather before allowing them to enter the Great Smokey Mountains National Park. Regardless of whether or not any of this was true, her message was clear: be prepared for cold, ice, and snow. The ranger at the Park entrance only checked our passes. The National Park Service had started requiring through-hikers to purchase permits to camp in the Smokies. It was an annoyance because we could not guarantee the dates of our arrival and departure. Fortunately, they were lax about enforcing the dates, as long as we had purchased a permit. Through-hikers are the only ones allowed to camp in the Smokies instead of using the shelters. Even then, we had to camp in a designated area near a shelter.

Slim and I met Danno at the Nantahala Outdoor Center, North Carolina, milepost 137. Danno had hiked all over the world. I learned more from observing him than I did from anyone else. He had an uncanny ability to look at his Trail guide—there are several books to choose from—and announce his arrival time at the next spot. He was always correct within a few minutes. I wonder if he sometimes sped up or slowed down to keep to his schedule. It didn't matter; he always arrived long before me. And Danno was a good man to have around. He had the most respectful way of approaching people, which produced results for us such as rides and favors. He would strike up a conversation with someone, then yell to us, "Hey guys, we have a ride."

Once Danno politely questioned a waitress about whether the dish he was served was what he had ordered. He softly asked, "Excuse me. Is this the …?" "No," she said, horrified, "that is not. I will get it right for you." You would have thought he was royalty the way she responded. If there had been hoops, I believe she would have leapt through them.

The waitress was being true to a code of honor: *take care of the trekkers.* If we were welcome at a business, they took good care of us. More than once I noticed our portions were larger, our salads had extra tomatoes, and the mashed potatoes or fries were heaping. We were dirty and odorous—once I cleared out the line at an ice cream stand, so they might require us to clean up before entering, but once inside we were treated well. Unfortunately, as we approached the larger cities in the North, we started to encounter places where we weren't welcome.

I kept up with Slim and Danno until Hot Springs, where I stayed to recover from a cold while they moved ahead. It was hard to see them go, but I was in no condition to continue.

Hot Springs was a good place to rest. It is one of the Trail Towns, designated by the Appalachian Conservancy as particularly welcoming to hikers. The Trail runs right through the middle of town, as it does in Damascus, Virginia, as well as Boiling Springs and Duncannon in Pennsylvania. Hot

Springs offers a choice of restaurants, a good outfitter, and shops to buy food and other supplies. Many hikers take time to relax at the famous springs there.

The 274 miles ending in Hot Springs had been a great adventure for me. My friends were moving ahead, I felt terrible, but I was enjoying the luxuries of civilization. If I had anything to prove, I had done it. Experienced trekkers told me I had the stuff to make it to Maine. Alone in a motel room in Hot Springs, for the first time, I thought about leaving the Trail. Yet, in that room, I found the motivation to continue trekking in the inspiration and opportunity it was providing me to write. I completed a couple of poems and began some others.

Intention
I write to make my words iron,
and I to be their iron wright
bending them to my will
with such masterly skill

that you see not tortured steel
but a sculptured garden gate
through which you pass to pause,
sit, rest, and contemplate.

Now, was that arrogant or what? Then, doubt questioned me, "Would any of my poems be good?" So I decided to set verbal challenges for myself, have fun, and see how it worked out. And so, this is what I do: I try to develop a poem around a sound, a phrase, or an image or just write some words and try to repeat the pattern. I enjoy the challenge and hope to improve with practice.

Inevitably, I began to think about a book—an audacious, vain notion. I had read trail journals written by others. I didn't have much to add to what had already been written. I wondered what kind of book it should be, so I started listing all the types of books I could think of, put similar books into groups and then, in a silly mood, I wrote the first of what I call my "Oh Poems."

Oh, to be a Book
Oh, to be a book!
But not a checkbook,
or a pocketbook;
and not a textbook,
schoolbook or notebook

not a test book,
bluebook or gradebook;
not a how-to book,
playbook or cookbook;
and not a workbook,
sketch book or art book;
and not a daybook,
scrapbook or yearbook;
not a storybook
and not a songbook,
not even your hymnbook;
and definitely
not your matchbook.
But the only book
you'll ever need,
the only book
you'll ever read
cover to cover.

I would write about my thoughts and emotions—not a trail journal in the traditional sense, but rather try to convey the feeling of the Trail and how that feeling changes over time. For the Trail is not one experience, but a series of a thousand moments.

Apologia

I am not a practiced, polished author
nor, until this, have I studied poetry,
prose or the performing arts. Despite
being a novice, with words I shall play,
making patterns in an effort to keep
order while remaining unconstrained
by conventions that might betray
the style of my voice. Nor will I efface
myself by imitating another.
Bound only to sound and meaning,
yet ever mindful of my arrogance
at controlling this conversation,
I endeavor to entertain and briskly
move forward.

Yet I am not an adventurer
with thrilling tales of heroic bravery
nor do I offer profound insight
into weighty matters that might convey
your attention into this book deeply
unless entertained and detained
by its integrity, you stay.
Thus in honesty, I shall embrace
both virtue and vice, success and failure.
I elect to write of common things
and write plainly, hoping to entrance
with heart spoken emotion
and by the plainspoken authenticity
of these words.

I write not to impress authors
but to be read by my brethren ordinary
folk and for my enjoyment. I write
to experiment, finding my own way
with words, not I pray rhyming cheaply
but setting words to order restrained
by the rules I set and then play,
playing to train my words to their place;
my inattentive ear to be a connoisseur;
my lazy tongue, discriminating;
and through repetition to advance
my skill at poetic expression
and by trial and error, test a boundary,
yet measured.

APPRAISAL

Triveni and I planned to meet in Las Vegas in August after she completed her commitment on the West Coast. We planned to take two weeks returning to Michigan, stopping at several national parks and places along the way where we would hike and camp.

When we parted in San Francisco, I joked to Triveni that it would be a good sign if I got off the plane in Las Vegas. She replied that it would be a good sign if she was there to meet me. I liked that she always gave back as good as she got from me. We enjoyed telling others about some witty phrase or comeback. We were proud of each other, repeating the repartee to friends. She teased me about being older, saying I didn't act like a 60-year old man.

The three-hour time difference between the Mid-West and Coast made it difficult for us to keep in touch. I would be going to sleep when it was early evening for her. When she woke up, I was already immersed in work and when I finished, she was still working. We spoke by phone a few times, emailed, and texted. We still considered ourselves to be together and in August, we both did show up at the airport in Las Vegas.

When we met, we had reached a natural decision point in our relationship: Would we stay together or not? It would be a risk either way. Before being separated by distance, we had a good relationship, the best and longest since my divorce. While we were apart, I had thought about her and our relationship, as I am certain, she had. Might I find someone else, better suited? What if we broke up later, after wasting dwindling good years on each other? Would I find someone then? Our meeting would be revealing. Could we pick up where we had left off?

After eight weeks apart, we slipped in next to each other as if our conversation had been momentarily interrupted when we stopped to fuel up and use the restroom. Just like we began, we were apart and then we were together, as simply as that. It felt like we had never been separated at all.

While in Las Vegas, we walked around the streets, visiting the casinos, seeing the sights, enjoying the buffets, dropping a few dollars into the slots, and watching the gamblers.

I Knew
Should have seen the comin' trouble,
but by then I was thinkin' double.
Double down and take the hit,
or play it safe and just sit?
Ai knew.... Ai knew.... Ai knew....
I knew before the card was turnin',
soon my luck would be endin'.
If not this hand then the next,
sooner or later I'd lose the bet.
Ai knew.... Ai knew.... Ai knew....
I knew I was playin' with more than chips.
Still I put it on the line
and played 'til all I had left was time
to count the harm I'd done.
Ai knew.... Ai knew.... Ai knew....
I knew it wasn't for the winnin'
but when the cards are all down,
and before the crowd can make a sound,
I swear you can hear hearts pound.
Ai knew.... Ai knew.... Ai knew....

I knew the hole was gettin' deeper
and I really should stop diggin'.
Not in a panic, more like a fever,
I had to get even.
Ai knew.... Ai knew.... Ai knew....
I knew I was riskin' more than money:
house and car, wife and kids.
I was bettin' my life and family.
Still I played that card.
Ai knew.... Ai knew.... Ai knew....
So go ahead, roll the dice once or twice.
Winnin' would be nice.
Better not count on it.
Better not bet your life on it.
But you know.... you know...
Ai knew.... Ai knew.... And now you know.

Leaving Las Vegas, we stopped at Hoover Dam and took the short tour before proceeding to tent near the Grand Canyon. In the morning, we planned to hike partway down into the Canyon.

The Grand Canyon was entertaining in an unexpected way. In my color-coordinated citified-hiking attire: hiking socks, khaki-colored hiking shorts with lots of pockets, matching synthetic shirt with slots under the arms and at my back, a wide-brimmed hat, and a daypack with dromedary water bladder on my back, I resembled a stylish magazine model version of a hiker. People kept asking me questions to which I didn't know the answers. Eventually one thought to ask, "Are you a ranger?" Once I replied that, "No," they stopped asking questions.

If fashionable, my attire wasn't well suited to the environment. I was over-dressed, sweating profusely, not only from the heat but from wearing too many clothes. Nowadays no one would mistake me for a model or a ranger. I have learned to wear as little as possible for the situation in order to reduce weight and to hike cool. A wide-brimmed hat or bandana, an ultra-thin shirt, light nylon shorts with two zippered pockets, socks and liner socks and trail runners, not boots unless winter, is all I wear. In colder weather, I change to a wool shirt and add compression shorts under my hiking shorts and eventually switch from shorts to pants. Muscles work better when they are cooler and the body sweats less, requiring less water, which is heavy.

Back at the Grand Canyon, it was a hot day, over 90 degrees. In the dry heat, we drank all of our water while hiking the 1.6 miles and 1,100 feet down the Bright Angel Trail to the first rest house. The sudden change in altitude, from 800 feet above sea-level in Michigan to 6,900 at the South Rim,

made me light-headed. At the top, I sat on a bench to recover while Triveni browsed in the gift shop.

The views of the Grand Canyon were incredible but sitting on the bench alone, my mind was on the holes in my life. The last of my children would soon be on her own. I could retire in a year. I would be free of responsibilities, but I was dissatisfied. My slate had been wiped clean, only to be covered by doodles. My life had lacked intimacy and meaning. I contrasted my life with and without Triveni.

Although I had kept busy with work, friends, and charity, I had missed Triveni while she was on the West Coast: the dates, going out for dinner, the quiet nights watching TV, and fighting over popcorn at a movie theater. I missed talking, joking, laughing with her and having her around. When we met in Las Vegas, I noticed that we had melded seamlessly, as if our time apart had never happened.

We camped at Cedar City, Utah, where it would be cooler due to its higher elevation than at Zion or Bryce National Parks, which would be day trips. However, heavy rain limited our activities at Zion.

HORSESHOE
BEND NEAR PAGE,
ARIZONA

Our trip was wonderful. There was much to see. Every bend in the road, every turn on a trail brought another astonishing view. Everything elicited a strong reaction, leading me to think of serious matters.

Bryce Canyon with its hoodoos defying gravity was my favorite place to hike. Hoodoos are oddly shaped pillars of stone. Shielded from above by hard rock, the layers of soft rock below erode thereby creating alternating bands of wide hard rock and narrow soft rock. Two hoodoos on a ridge made me think of friends who had died. A friend I had known since the second grade died in 1999. His illness and death had reinforced my decision to work from home and spend more time with my children. Other friends died during the next decade. Several more had near misses. It was a dangerous period for my friends. I counted seven occassions, illnesses, accidents, and near-accidents that might have ended my own life. How long would my own luck hold?

A Friend

I stood on a mountain with a friend
and thought that time would never end,
then there was only one.
How long until there are none?

There always was a feeling of failure and a nagging thought that I was failing a test of my commitment, a choice I hadn't been ready to make.

From Cedar City, we drove next to Moab, Utah, stopping near Capitol Reef National Park along the way to see the petroglyphs. At Capitol Reef, I hiked down a canyon alone while Triveni waited back at the car. She said it was too hot and, after the Grand Canyon and Bryce, she wanted to rest.

I had time to think while I was alone. I had known men and women with elaborate romantic pasts. Some had multiple marriages. Others always seemed to have someone around, if never for long. *Were they incapable of maintaining a relationship?* Now I found myself joining them. The women who had been married several times began to look downright respectable. At least, they had been married. There had been too many women in my life.

TWO HOODOO "FRIENDS" AT BRYCE CEDAR CITY, UTAH

We all must have a secret demon that we battle. For some it is drugs or alcohol, perhaps gambling, envy, love of money, power, fame, or lust. I remembered a young woman who had told me that she was like an alcoholic with men. Alcoholics say one drink is too many and a dozen too few. She said, if she had sex with one man, she would follow with man after man. She didn't know whether she was capable of a lasting monogamous relationship.

I was not like this sex-addicted woman, but had found myself to be easily distracted by other females. An attraction seized my attention. Yet, if I were distracted and then looked back, the allure vanished, like a firecracker that had exploded and then disappeared into the night sky, leaving me to wonder what the commotion had been all about. What could have been so appealing? That was the test I had adopted, wait a while to see whether someone else appealed to me or I remained interested in a particular woman. I had not been distracted even while Triveni and I had been apart.

After a few months of dating, the woman and I would stop to assess each other. There were always reasons to break up. I discovered that some women and, I presume, some men, purposely would end a relationship after a few months because they didn't want to complicate their lives with anything more serious than companionship. They were content to have fun but at the first discussion or question about "where is this going?" their response was to disappear.

Usually though, there were something that we had overlooked until suddenly it began to annoy us. There always were imperfections and differences to work through, not to mention balancing all the other parts our lives. Typically, it wasn't an important issue that caused us to reconsider our relationship, but rather something small, a wayward comment, a disagreement, an assumption or a slight, perhaps unintentional, that made us question whether this was a good idea after all. Wanting some space, we might take a little break and that led us to step back. Sometimes we just seemed to slow down, like a roller coaster coming to a stop, and finding no reason to stay in, we got out.

At these times, when we knew our relationship wouldn't last, either the woman or I ended it. In almost perfect symmetry, for every relationship I ended, it seemed a woman ended one with me. It didn't matter who ended the relationship, we both sensed that something essential was missing. It wasn't the real thing.

Rarely was there a contentious blowup, just a breakup: good-bye and good luck with your life. We hadn't invested that much in each other, and perhaps that was the underlying cause of our breakup. Sometimes, one of us just stopped calling or returning calls. No need to explain; at our ages, we'd both been here before, we were moving on with our separate lives without each other.

A few women needed to vent during a breakup, as if needing to assign blame to me. Above all, it must not be seen to be their fault, when in fact it was "us." I didn't see much benefit to this kind of a discussion, as it only created bad feelings and burned bridges. Interestingly, these women had all been divorced from men who had cheated on them. I never did cheat on any of these women, nor to my knowledge, did any cheat on me.

Rarely did we stay in touch for long after we broke up. Once you have had sex, it's hard to turn that dial down. Besides, when one of us became involved someone else, that person wouldn't be comfortable that we remained in contact with former lovers.

Not that breaking up was easy. There always was a feeling of failure and a nagging thought that I was failing a test of my commitment, a choice I hadn't been ready to make. I felt that way even though I wasn't the only one who was unwilling to make a commitment.

During that walk alone down the canyon at Capitol Reef, I thought about my life since my divorce. My marriage had fallen apart and I hadn't been in a relationship that lasted more than several months until Triveni. Yet, I wasn't content with short-term relationships. I wanted something more from life. I wanted someone to share my life with; someone I could rely on;

someone who would stick with me through the good times and bad; someone to make memories with and to grow old with. I wanted to be all of those things for her as well.

I thought about how long it had taken me to find someone I would consider as a potential wife. And no, I wasn't getting any younger. What if this was my last chance at finding a partner? We were doing well together. We had a shot at something more lasting than another short-term relationship.

Never Thought
Never thought what a woman wanted,
long as I got what I wanted,
I was happy.
I thought I was happy.

Never cared whose heart got broken.
Just said the words that needed to be spoken,
I'd get lucky.
I thought I was lucky.

Never thought 'bout wrong or right,
long as I could spend the night,
it was easy.
I thought love was easy.

Then came a thought that continued to haunt me:
what if all my hits and scores added up to naught?
Somethin' was missin'.
what was I missin'?

It wasn't that my heart was broken
or lack of words that might be spoken.
I was tired of winnin'.
What was I winnin',
when no one was playin'?
No one was playin' anymore.

Wasn't that there were so many,
less than I wanted and less than I might've,
still more than I should've,
more than I should've.

Tried to change, but my reputation preceded me.
Women thought they could see right through me.

Women could see right through me.
It wasn't easy anymore,
no, not easy anymore.

Wish I could say this had a happy ending.
Yet, maybe someday a woman will take a chance on me
and this time I'll know I'm lucky.
This time, I'll know I'm lucky.

And if I can make her happy, make her laugh and smile,
so she thinks she's lucky and sticks around for a while,
then I'll be happy too.
At last, I'll be happy.

And if we're both happy, maybe we'll move in together.
I know I'll have to change; it won't be easy for her.
No, not easy.
Lord knows, it won't be easy for her.

Love is never easy, but you take your chance
and maybe you'll get lucky. You'll both be lucky
and at last, you'll be happy.
At last you'll both be happy.
(continued)

I thought about Triveni as a person. I took my time running through the pros and cons. There was strong chemistry between us.

Legend
Our love will be like a legend,
unwritten,
lost in time, forever hidden,
forgotten,
not a story of passion
but a lesson,
a caring admonition
for children,
and those hoping for the resurrection
of affection,
and to others an inspiration,
but a story,
nay, an epic known only to you and me.

She was kind to others and had many friends, many more than me. She was intelligent as well as athletic. We differed about both politics and religion. Unlike some women I had met, she was not materialistic and managed her finances very well. On the other hand, she needed to continue working for many more years, while I was contemplating retirement. She had been divorced for a few years, and I was her first serious relationship since then. Her divorce had been contentious and she remained bitter about that. I was concerned that she was still working through those emotions.

I questioned myself, *Was this the real thing, or was it only the excitement of being together again?* Did I want us to stay together or not, and what did she want?

Into a Pool

I dove deeply into a pool thinking of you.
Immersing myself completely,
submerged I swam its length and breadth,
emerging only to catch my breath.

Resting along its side,
avoiding conversation,
I contemplated my relationship with you,
assessing the nature of my obsession.

It is an infatuation, that it is true,
fueled by a physical attraction;
I cannot deny the spark
that moves me to action.

For once, trying to be wise,
and unwilling to be captured by passion
that only intensifies,
I consider other qualities about you:

there is my appreciation
for the consideration you show me,
and, growing with each interaction,
my deepening admiration

for your kindness toward others,
and the strength of your character,
confirmed by your choices
on life's great decisions and daily matters.

I recognize imperfections in you,
your agile mind decides too quickly
while I deliberate until certain;
you enjoy being contrary

to those earnest ones who haven't a clue
of the game you are playing with them;
and you have so many things to do,
I wonder whether there is room for anyone;

It feels like we're always negotiating;
and while you seem content,
sometimes I think you're just waiting
for something to begin or something to end.

And yet from our first walk,
when suddenly the world lit,
and I turned in shock to look at you,
tricked, for once in a lifetime, by sunlight?

Immersing myself completely,
I dove into a pool thinking it was you.
Emerging I discovered an ocean
that might take a lifetime to traverse.

If you had been fishing,
and I know you were not,
the hook has been set
and I am happily caught.

It was time to make a commitment.

A WONDROUS VIEW IN THE GREAT SMOKEY MOUNTAINS NATIONAL PARK

CHAPTER 4: *Dreams*

Could we be fools,
like anxious adolescents,
wanting to believe
in love constant,
and thus eager accomplices
to our ensnarement?

SELF-ASSURANCE

By Hot Springs, I thought, *I might actually make it to Katahdin.* I'd hiked several hundred miles through bad weather, rough terrain, and had overcome equipment failures and mistakes.

Along the way, I had gained confidence. Sure, I had made mistakes; everyone did. I took a wrong turn, easy to do in some places, but found my way back. I ran short of water, but made do. Something broke and I fixed it or found a work-around. Trekking was a crash course on self-reliance and problem solving. It built self-confidence and instilled a sense of calm, level-headedness in the face of adversity.

Although it might not sound like it, I did some things right. My sleeping bag repelled water, not a flood, but enough to keep me dry under snow and through wind-blown rain. A small pouch attached to my belt held my camera and kept snacks handy. A 12-hour sunscreen, a lubricant popular with cyclists to reduce chafing, and heavy-duty bug repellent protected my skin. Wool shirts proved wise in the cold, wet weather. I pre-treated all of my clothes, boots, and hat with permethrin to repel insects. Once when walking through a cloud of flies, others commented that there were none around me. "I smell so bad, even bugs won't come near," I replied.

I spent more time deciding which form of underwear, if any, to wear while hiking than any other garment. There were two issues to balance: the retention of moisture and chafing. Underwear held rain and sweat against the skin, promoting skin irritations. Wearing no underwear allowed moisture to evaporate quickly, but increased the risk of chafing from the rubbing of skin on skin and zipper burn.

I learned from other, more experienced hikers. I put my sweaty hiking clothes inside my sleeping bag at night. They would be dry and warm in the morning.

As underwear, compression shorts worked best. They prevented chaffing but once wet, the constant dampness irritated my skin. Moreover, the compression shorts needed to be washed out at night before they could be worn again. One pair, which I was wearing when I sat in a puddle to avoid falling, needed to be machine washed in hot water before I could wear them without developing a rash. Thus I needed to carry at least two pair: one pair to wear while the other dried.

Thanks to my dentist who insisted, under threat of excommunication, I took my battery-powered tooth flosser with me. When using it, I didn't have to put my dirty, possibly contaminated hands near my mouth. Following an online tip, I set dots of toothpaste out to dry. They became gummy and easily rolled into balls. I would chew one after a meal until it dissolved. I returned to my dentist without controversy.

I cautiously filtered or chemically treated water, especially when using water from streams or pools. Who knew whether those sources were contaminated? The water from streams with moss growing and the springs high in the mountains were supposed to be safe to drink, but why take the chance? One bad episode would outweigh the effort required to be safe. In 2014, a young man had been diagnosed with giardia, which causes diarrhea. Needless to say, he was being more careful after that torturous experience.

I grew to love the mountain springs providing cool, clear water even though I still filtered or treated it.

Spring
God might be many things
but I like him best
when I think of him as a spring:

a hot spring
on a cold winter day,
where I can rest,
its warmth seeping into my core
and staying with me
when I step into the cold;

a cool spring
on a hot summer day,
where, by sun and heat stressed,
I pause to drink and restore
my vitality;

or a piped spring
above a waterway,
by far the best
place to find clean water to pour
over me.

For a spring
is a grace and I always
leave feeling blessed
and when I go to church
I leave refreshed.

I learned from other, more experienced hikers. I put my sweaty hiking clothes inside my sleeping bag at night. They would be dry and warm in the morning. Lightweight bottles from sports drinks replaced the heavier, more durable camping bottles. At every town, hostel, or store, I purchased two new liter bottles of a sports drink to use until the next store. My expensive sock liners were replaced by the cheapest, thinnest nylon socks that could be found almost anywhere.

My tarp took too long to set up, but pre-tied slipknots and carabineers that could be quickly tightened cut the time required. A light version of a house wrap used building new homes served as a ground cover to protect my tent and sleeping pad against puncture and as an additional barrier to moisture. On frigid nights, my toes were always cold so I started wearing my gloves on my feet. It worked; my toes stayed comfortably warm.

In an effort to reduce weight, I discarded unused items but added others: two small flashlights; two small, sharp blades; and two bandannas. One flashlight I kept in a pocket of my sleeping bag—always handy at night. One blade I used with food, the other I kept in my first aid kit. The accumulation of salts from sweat on the bandanna irritated my forehead. So, I wore one bandanna while the other dried after being rinsed out.

The diciest challenge I faced occurred in the Smokies. Coming down an icy trail, I slid toward its downslope edge, catching myself against a slender tree. I was at a bend in the trail. Forward or back on the Trail was pure ice without a tree nearby to grab. I could not step down because I didn't trust that the steep, damp slope would hold me. The surface had melted, but the underneath was still frozen. The surface might slip away if I stepped onto it. I wouldn't slide far before hitting a tree or boulder.

Across the trail, the uphill side was a bit flatter and still covered in snow. If I could get there, I could walk my way out on it. Twice, I tried, and each time slid back, my feet slamming against the narrow base of the tree. I couldn't keep bumping up against that thin tree. Sooner or later, it would give.

On the upside slope, I spotted a small stump. I extended a trekking pole to its maximum length, then reached across the trail to lasso the stump with the strap of the pole. Carefully I pulled myself to safety then walked out. I felt pretty good about being able to walk out, instead of crawling, until I slipped on the wet ice and fell on my butt again.

By Damascus, Virginia, my speed and stamina had improved. I timed myself again, learning my maximum speed to be 2.8 mph over mixed terrain, almost twice my starting speed of 1.5 mph on the first day ascending Springer, but could not sustain that speed into the afternoon. I was faster downhill and on stretches of easier terrain, but only 1.5 mph or less going uphill. I could cover almost 12 miles in a morning and when I wanted, last 12 hours. Twenty-plus mile days were possible, if exhausting. I was a lean walking machine, the old 1950s model.

The Trail ahead promised to be rewarding. There were legendary mountains to hike, vistas, towns, and hostels to visit. There would be challenges ahead. I would make more mistakes. A thousand possibilities awaited me, both good and bad. Yet, I started to believe I could make it. It was only a matter of will power, care, and luck.

HOPEFULNESS

In 2010, while I walked down the canyon at Capitol Reef National Park alone, I thought about people whose spouses had died. The widows and widowers had memories that sustained them through their new lives without their spouses. While they mourned their loss, they seemed consoled by the fact that their spouse had died loving them, whereas those of us who were divorced were a more mixed lot. We might be bitter, or if not happy, relieved. Even those of us who had a good divorce, as good as a divorce can be, were never comfortable with how our marriages ended. Since our divorce, my ex-wife and I had gradually reconciled, recognizing the good in each other. Yet I hadn't healed from my divorce until one of my daughters said, "I don't think we were harmed by the divorce, because we had a strong relationship with both you and Mom." Still, there remains a difference between those who lost a loved one and those who lost love.

Queen

Once upon a time
I feel in love with a queen
or so she seemed to be
when she wore her widowhood
like a golden crown
to keep us from disturbing
her wonderful dream:

A queen in the memories
of her prince and then king.
And this was my quandary:
was it this noble queen
that captivated me,
or had I fallen in love
not with her but with her dream,
or was I the one dreaming,
dreaming of what might be?

How would you have counseled me:
should I have been content to dream
or should I have risked waking
by asking this regal queen
to share in my dream?

On the drive to Moab, Utah, in 2010, I thought about one friend who had recently died and how he had lived his final years. He had quit his job as a consultant. He could not initiate contact with his former clients due to his legal agreement to not compete with his former employer. When a certain client called him, she asked why he had quit his job when she relied upon his support. He told her, "Because we can't date while you are my client." He found a new job, and they married and remained together until he died in 2008.

My thoughts turned away from my past, to the future and what I hoped it would bring. My friend's leaving his job had been a grand romantic

statement of his feelings for his future wife. If I could not be so grand as to leave my employment, I would hope to be as romantic in a proposal. *Was I actually thinking of marrying Triveni?* We had talked about marriage, someday, maybe. It was what we both wanted long-term. People assumed we were married.

At Arches National Park, we planned to walk out to Double Arch. I remained silent on the way there. My heart beat quickly with emotion and from hiking in the dry heat, while I debated with myself one last time: *Should I ask Triveni to marry or not? Was it the excitement of being together again? Perhaps I should wait. And if she accepts, what might happen to us?* You hope for the best and do what you can, but you never know how a marriage will go.

What if she refused? During our time apart, she must have thought about me and our relationship. Had she decided to move on and was only waiting to get home to tell me? It didn't seem that way. She was happy to see me and we were behaving as before our separation.

When we arrived, I handed my camera to a French hiker and asked him to take our picture. I positioned us under Double Arch, then turned Triveni sidewise to face me. I surprised her by kneeling. I decided to keep it simple, a few words. "I don't want us to be apart again," I told her.

And then, "Will you marry me?"

Three Wishes

If I were granted three magical wishes,
the first I would give to you
in the hope that you might wish,
as I, to spend my life loving you

so that with the second, I could wish
for us a long life together
and from the third ask,
we always should be happy with each other.

If, choosing to be unselfish,
you chose to end war, famine, or poverty,
I would ask, "What should I wish?"
hoping one wish might be saved for you and me,

proving your love for me
and showing I am not taken for granted,
that while saving humanity,
those closest to you will be attended.

If you were to ask for worldly things,
riches, luxury, fame, and power,
or foolish, girlish things,
eternal, youthful beauty, parties, and admirers;

Or, should I be woefully mistaken
and you were to wish for another,
I would cheer my liberation
from a merciless abductor,

then I would use my remaining wishes,
first to mend my broken heart
until free from disappointment and anguish,
I would ask for a new start.

I do not have any magical wishes,
only this one life to give to you,
risking that you might wish,
as I, to spend your life loving me.

If this is not what you want to be,
I will thank you for your honesty
and for allowing me to believe
that love remains a possibility,

but should this prove to be an error,
only time to mend my broken heart,
until finding with another
true love and a fresh start.

❧

It had been a short walk to Double Arch, but it had been the longest walk of my life, with my final decision, the proposal and her acceptance, all within an hour or two. So much happened so quickly. Later she told me that, because I was silent and withdrawn that day, she thought there was something wrong. I might have been preparing to break up with her. Yet, Triveni entered my dream by answering my proposal with a "Yes."

I stood and we kissed. She had accepted the risk, taking a chance on the two of us. She later used one of the pictures of us for the background on her laptop screen. We called friends and families, who were surprised but happy for us.

Our decision to continue our romance included a large measure of hopes and wishes. An engagement is not a time when one thinks of everything that might go wrong. No, we thought only about the good things that we hoped the future would bring.

Your Only Lover

I wanta be your only lover,
the one you choose above all others,
never regrettin', never doubtin',
never wonderin' what might you be missin'.

I wanta learn your do's and don'ts,
be on the inside of all your jokes,
hear your wishes, dreams, and hopes,
lift you up when you're all out of rope.

I wanta be the one you turn to first,
when things are at their very worst;
when there's no one else left to ask,
the one you think to call at last.

I wanta chase and catch you, tickle and tease you,
hug and kiss, hold and squeeze you,
make love, cuddle, and talk for hours
in that special time, we'll call "ours."

I wanta hear you singin' in the mornin',
catch you in the kitchen dancin',
surprise you by jumpin' in
even though I'm not much for dancin'.

I'll be with you every day,
be there on your good days,
stick with you through the bad.
I'll be the best friend you ever hoped to have.

And when we're old and gray,
sittin' on a park bench, holdin' hands,
rememberin' all our yesterdays,
thinkin',
"Now, that was the way love should be."

We were aware of issues that would need to be resolved before we could marry. There were many details to work out before merging our two lives, such as the seven years age difference complicating employment and retirement schedules as well as families, holidays, housing, and many more that would appear. There would be questions and differences we would have to confront but we were older, more experienced, and possibly wiser and those issues lay in the future.

Right now, we had made a commitment to continue moving forward. We might still have doubts and anxieties about our future. Anyone would. But that night, we celebrated.

Let's go out for Dinner
Let's go out for dinner,
'n' stop in at a bar.
You go put on a pretty dress,
while I clean up the car.

Let's go out on the town,
have a good time, make it last,
ride with the top down
and drive too fast.

There's no need to hurry,
no need to rush.
Take your time getting ready.
There'll be time enough for us.

And, if that bar has music
and the moment seems right,
I might ask you to dance,
just so I can hold you tight.

Let's get away from this crowd,
drive out in the country,
act like we're young again
and play our music too damn loud.

Let's go down by the river.
Don't forget to bring a blanket.
If you start to shiver,
you can put on my jacket.

Let's hold hands while we walk,
stick to the paths through the park,
find a quiet spot,
turn and kiss in the dark.

Let's look up at the heavens,
count all the stars,
search for constellations
and wait for that meteor show.

I'll wrap you in my arms
while we listen to nature sing
to the music from those stars,
or is that the magic between us?

Our last stop was at Rocky Mountain National Park. We were on top of the world.

ALONG THE DRIVE ONTO THE KENAI PENINSULA, ALASKA

Though not a trick,
More like an arrangement:
each needing the other
to some precious purpose,
but once accomplished,
then to what end, commitment?

COLLABORATION

While trekking, I grew to appreciate the restorative power of human companionship. The Trail might temporarily reinvigorate with a surprisingly wondrous sight, but one begins to hunger for the company of another human. For a trek is debilitating to the spirit as well as the body; one cannot complete a trek without periodic infusions of kind conversation.

Most trekkers, myself included, go alone, hoping to make friends along the way. They might only hike up a hill together, chatting as they go. It is easier climbing while speaking with someone. It hurries you along and passes the time. I met Cruise and Corn Dog that way. Outside of Hiawassee, Georgia, I enjoyed a long conversation with a "new age" hiker about religion, philosophy, love, and life as we climbed. At one point, he told me about how he was drawn to a certain place where he found a rock that he placed by his bed after which he never had back pain again. He told that story to illustrate his larger point that we were where we needed at that moment, if only we could only figure out why. I liked his message even though I thought his story was hooey. *Was he pulling my leg?*

It was a wryly amusing walk because at times he was walking, if not backwards, sidewise up the hill, so we could continue talking, while I struggled to keep to him. Later, I had similar experiences in Virginia and again in New Jersey with younger hikers walking sidewise ahead of me while we had engaging conversations about life, the Trail, and other weighty and trivial matters.

Much as the dogs loved being on the Trail, it was as hard for them as it was us.

Eventually, trekkers found someone they liked, who had a compatible agenda, and saw the world similarly. Not that they hiked together all day, but they started out in the morning and ended up at night and if one didn't show, the other noticed. They might meet for lunch. If they encountered Trail Magic, they'd save a bit for their partner. They encouraged and supported each other. Slim, Danno, and I even enjoyed meals that one person couldn't carry by dividing the food among us before we left town.

After being left behind at Hot Springs to recover, I was surprised to catch up with Slim and Danno at Erwin, Tennessee, milepost 340. I had stopped at a meadow south of town for lunch when I heard someone call my name. It was Slim?! He warned me not to approach him. He was slack-packing south in order to make up the miles he had skipped to go into town when he caught a mild case of norovirus. He didn't want to infect me.

Slim and Danno were sharing a room at the hostel in Erwin. I managed to stay in a cabin by myself because all the other cabins contained sick hikers or were fully occupied. Other friends were in town, including my first friends, Cruise and Corn Dog, and Waffles, who was a young man I got to know in Hot Springs where I had lingered to recover from a cold. He was a pleasant fellow who was hiking before starting a career. At best, we all looked scruffy and unkempt, but somehow Waffles always appeared well-dressed. After he purchased a new hat that I liked, I teased him, calling him "The Stylish Waffles." He took it with good humor. Our stay at Erwin became a reunion. We took a group photo of six of us who had started on the same day. When we left Erwin, I kept up with Slim and Danno until Marion, Virginia, at milepost 531 when Slim left to attend a family event and Danno sped ahead.

After Slim and Danno, I hiked for a while with HoBo and then later with Otto, Olive Oyl, and Wet Bag. Otto had been Danno's first companion. He was an enthusiastic young man fresh out of the military and fun to be around. Wet Bag was a young man who had just graduated from college. He was a friend of Olive Oyl, and they hiked most of the Trail together. He was quiet, thoughtful and considerate.

Trekking in 2014 was an experience entirely different from 2013. I started at Daleville, Virginia, far ahead of the crowd back at Springer Mountain in Georgia. The few trekkers I encountered were on a schedule, some racing to be first to Katahdin in Maine. Almost all stopped to talk for a while, sometimes deciding to stay the night before speeding off in the morning. We all hungered for conversation and companionship.

Surprisingly, I found myself lonelier when more hikers started showing up. They had been hiking around each other for a long time, and I was an outsider. It was wise of them to be cautious around a stranger. Besides, I was slow and they would probably never see me again. Another hiker confided to me that he had started leaving notes in the registers asking for someone to please talk with him. Some would realize a trekker's loneliness and be courteously friendly, but most avoided or ignored you.

I did have a great week hiking with Up Hill. He had through-hiked several years before and came out for a month. After my difficulties in 2013, I was being overly cautious. Up Hill encouraged me to overcome my doubts, helping me to recover my confidence. We hiked 107 miles in six and a half days.

After Up Hill, I spent a couple days around two young women and a young man. We commemorated crossing the point marking 1,000 miles to Katahdin with pictures of fingers making the number 1,000. Even though I hardly got to know them, I was saddened when they forged ahead of me.

It is important to enjoy trail companionship while it lasts, because sooner or later, companions separate. One of you might take a zero day or go into town to meet a friend or partner. Chances were you'd meet again further up the Trail but then again maybe not. Trekkers hiked alone for long periods.

DOGS ON THE TRAIL

Some hikers brought their dogs for companionship and protection. Trekking dogs got used to being around strangers and there was a nice, warm feeling when a dog, recognizing me, greeted me with a wagging tail.

I'm a dog lover and enjoyed having dogs on the Trail with us. The trail dogs sensed that I liked them. One night in a hostel, when a young woman didn't let her dog onto her bed, the dog jumped into bed with me. I continued sleeping soundly through the night, warm and cozy. In the morning, the owner was apologetic. I said, "No problem," then added the dog hadn't been my first choice. Thankfully, everyone laughed and that was that.

One woman slept with her dog in her hammock. She said the dog wrapped its paws around her. What with the possibility of ticks, fleas, and who knows what else, I didn't think this was a good idea, but she said it was fine. In town, her dog waited by the door of the hostel or store she was in, eager to get back to the trail.

Much as the dogs loved being on the Trail, it was as hard for them as it was us. One hiker lost his dog; the woods are not a place for a friendly, innocent city dog to be alone.

I did not like the day-hikers who let their dogs run free. At times, I had to threaten to stab or beat charging, barking dogs with my trekking poles. Owners objected to my defensive moves, but I wasn't about to take a chance.

After my return from the Appalachian Trail in 2013, a woman asked me if I had found God there. Her question annoyed me and all I could respond was a scornful "No." In the great outdoors, one cannot help but think about God, the universe, and creation because nature is expansive, powerful, and majestic. Removed from the safety and security of civilization, we appear small, frail, and insignificant.

The more remote the location, the more aware I became of the fragility of my existence, especially when I was alone. There were hundreds of opportunities to be injured or killed in the wilderness. I might drown crossing a stream. In 2014, the first time my pole collapsed was when I was on a log crossing a quickly flowing stream. I put a pole into the water to steady myself, then bent over with the pole collapsing into itself. I thought, *Wow, that stream is deeper than I thought.* When I pulled the pole out, I saw it had collapsed. I did not fall in because by then, I had learned not to put my full weight onto a pole, lest it slip and I lose my balance. Falling into that swiftly flowing steam would have been a problem; if not by hitting my head on a rock, by drenching my clothes and gear on a cold spring day.

Lightning might strike. At Max Patch Bald, North Carolina, a young man and I ate while watching a thunderstorm approaching from the east. In a game of chicken, we debated when to leave, until he won: I stood up, and then we both hurried away. A young woman had been killed by lightning there a few years earlier. We agreed it was a shame to leave Max Patch because we would have liked to have spent the night and vowed to camp there someday.

A bad fall was always a risk. A misstep might take me down a slope or into a crevice where no one would hear my calls or ever think to look for me after I died from thirst. At times, a limb or a tree fell nearby, especially unnerving at night. Sometimes people are killed by bears, snakes, or other animals. All extremely unlikely events; millions of people hike every year to nothing more than blisters and sprained ankles, but bad things do happen, even sometimes to well-seasoned hikers.

I prayed for my safety and that of others, stopped in at a Christian church when in town, and tried to be more mindful of my actions. Superstitiously, I hoped that my good behavior might protect me from harm.

I had been raised as a Roman Catholic but ranged back and forth from a lapsed Catholic to a recovered Catholic, while investigating other religions, until deciding that Christianity was the only religion that made any sense to me. If there is a God, He Himself must come among us to show us the way, lest His message be distorted by those who would profit from religion.

When I returned to civilization, I quickly became complacent. At home, I have always walked carefully on snow and ice, washed my hands regularly,

What about civilization had made me less observant? Civilization had secured safety, security, and health for most of us.

and so forth and I was thankful for all the benefits of modern life. But my "partnership" with God—if I prayed to thank Him and behaved, he would protect me—weakened. Back home, I faltered I might skip church, forget to pray, and was generally less mindful of my behavior.

What about civilization had made me less observant? Civilization had secured safety, security, and health for most of us. Why had this security, and the implicit assumption of the continued success of civilization, lulled me into complacency?

The woman's question about God reminded me of how I had felt at Bryce Canyon before becoming engaged, where the walls had resembled cathedrals and temples. Perhaps a better question might be asked:

What about Civilization?
Although they might deny it,
claiming emotion has nothing
to do with it,
I imagine it must be easier
to be an atheist
or at least an agnostic

in small places
like an apartment
in a building
made of steel, concrete, and brick,
with good heating and a shower or tub
with plenty of hot water to soak in,
with markets nearby
where goods magically appear
and restaurants that deliver.
Who thinks about God
when the pizza man will deliver?
And in the morning,
reliable garbage pick-up.

Easier in secure places
like a nice house on a quiet street
in a decent neighborhood
with good schools,
a street where the front yards are neat,
backyards have grills,
patios, and pools
and in the basements,
exercise bikes and treadmills;
to find it reassuring
to be in a great metropolis
or university town
surrounded by accomplished people,
and the great works
and rules of men.

Easier in a country
where the government
takes such good care of us,
where education is free,
with food stamps and Medicaid
for the needy,
Medicare and social security
for the elderly,
9-1-1 to call in an emergency,
and now health care for the rest of us
and all of it paid for us.

Easier now that science
can do damn near anything:
help the blind man to see,
and the deaf man to hear,
cure and prevent almost every disease,
even control the climate,
and stop the oceans rising.
I read it on the Internet
and heard it on the TV.
Almost nothing beyond our abilities.
All we need to do
is spend a little more money.
Gotta love that science.

But let's not waste the day
talking about God and religion.
Just look at that mountain,
reaching way up into the sky.

For my return to the Trail in 2014, I drove most of the way to my starting point at Daleville, Virginia, through rain, unable to see much of Ohio and West Virginia outside my windows. As I approached Daleville, the rain stopped. I glimpsed blue ridges through thin clouds draped over them like lace. I was recharged and rejuvenated, eager to restart the Trail. It reminded me of the boost to my morale that I had received from well-run hostels, Trail Magic, and visual surprises along the Trail.

HOSTELS

While hiking the Appalachian Trail, you need to go into a town periodically to resupply, shower, do laundry, and eat as much town food as you could. One large young man reportedly consumed twelve cheeseburgers one long afternoon. I could never stomach that much at one sitting. Instead, I fit in four or five meals each day in town.

For most trekkers, it was too expensive to stay in hotels, motels, or bed and breakfasts along the way and eat only in restaurants. Instead, most stayed at hostels, which ranged from minimal bunkhouses to rather respectable private accommodations. Usually, laundry service was available as well as a ride into and back from a nearby town to resupply. Most hostels had a regular bathroom, although some relied on privies and outdoor showers. Almost all provided a microwave and a refrigerator stocked with frozen pizzas, frozen sandwiches, ice cream, fruit, drinks and snacks, and a selection of personal care items, all available for a fee paid on the honor system. Some hostels included full kitchens where hikers could cook more complete and satisfying meals. In addition, hostels presented an opportunity to socialize with other trekkers, often over drinks.

Running a hostel might seem like a good way to make some money, but it's not. Business is extremely seasonal. A crowd of hikers comes through for a month or two and then they are gone. Then too most trekkers are young and would much rather spend their limited funds partying. While there might be money to make during the trekking season, it could not be relied upon as a primary source of income.

An unfortunate side effect of through-hiking was that some trekkers become focused upon their own epic quest at the expense of others. Some thought nothing of cheating businesses and hostellers. A few walked out on tabs at restaurants and bars, sticking the waitress with the bill, or raided the snack bars and refrigerators at hostels, then underreported what they'd

taken. Sometimes, though, it wasn't certain that the guilty parties were through-hikers. Businesses shared information up and down the Trail via the Internet; some trekkers were turned away from hostels.

So why do people run hostels along the Trail? I've talked to several hostellers who told me that running a hostel was a gift, an act of love for the Trail and the community of hikers. It was rewarding in many ways, not just financially. Of course, they had to make ends meet. No one could afford to subsidize hiker after hiker, and most hostellers walked a thin financial line. What separated the good facilities from the bad was those who did it because they loved the Trail. I think especially of hostels near Hiawassee, Erwin, Roan Mountain, Damascus, Waynesboro, Front Royal, Palmerton and one in a glen near Pearisburg, Virginia.

Hostel
When you were young, did you dream
of a simple life on a farm,
a farm with happy dogs and cats,
a place to grow your own food,
to keep a few pigs for meat,
some goats and a cow for milk,
and for eggs, ducks, and chickens:
a farm set, of course, in a dell?

Below runs a peaceful stream;
above, your cabin and barn;
on the porch, a welcome mat;
inside, blissful quietude,
a wood stove provides heat
to a great room where quilts,
couches, and good books beckon:
rest and read, to a weary clientele.

In the hallway, hot coffee and cream
with more drinks and breads fresh and warm
and leftovers as snacks;
from the kitchen, aromas exude,
tonight you will overeat
and feel no guilt.
At last, the mistress in her floured apron
emerges to ring the dinner bell.

If you, like I, allowed young dreams to die
but now cannot remember why:
did we give them serious thought,
did we lack the fortitude
or simply dismiss them as quaint and obsolete,
and did they like an untended flower wilt?
When you think of dreams long ago forsaken,
find solace in a place where dreams do indwell.

TRAIL MAGIC

When I was tired, when I was unhappy, when I was down, when I really needed something, Trail Magic appeared and always proved to be exactly what I needed at the time. On May 17, 2013, the stiches fastening a shoulder strap to my backpack came apart. While I sat by a forest road wondering how to reattach the strap so I could continue, along came a young woman. She saw I was holding a needle and thread in one hand, the strap in the other hand with the empty backpack stretched across my lap. She offered to make the repair for me, explaining that she was an artist-seamstress from Poland. What were the odds an expert at sewing heavy fabric might show up within minutes of my needing her assistance? She wasn't a trekker. She had come to America to visit friends. They had gone for an overnight hike and were to be picked up at the forest road where I was sitting in a few minutes. If my strap had lasted a bit longer, we would have passed by each other, or if they had

A MAGICAL PLACE
BELOW THE BLUE
RIDGE PARKWAY,
VIRGINIA

arranged to be picked up earlier, we would have never met. What a fortuitous convergence of beneficiary and benefactor!

"Trail Angels," as they are called, are individuals, a family, or a group. Church groups and scout troops sometimes left Trail Magic for through-hikers along the Trail. Some Trail Angels had been through-hikers themselves, or had wanted to be, but for some reason, could not. Others might have had a family member who had been a through-hiker. Others were just kind souls. All were united in their compassion: they knew through-hikers were often in need and they wanted to help.

There are many wonderful stories I could tell about Trail Magic. There were offers of candy, snacks, fruit, soda, rides into and out of town, people taking me into their homes, first aid, and supplies of all sorts.

Some Trail Angels provided picnics, setting up grills, tables, and chairs. There might be grilled chicken, hamburgers, and hot dogs. A hunter and his wife, who had planned to through-hike, but couldn't for some unstated reason, put on barbecues for through-hikers using their supplies, cooking gear, and butchered venison, beaver, and other meats (caught by the hunter), which they brought from Michigan. Once I arrived at a lake to find my friends had saved the last piece of BBQ chicken for me. Relaxing in a lawn chair, chatting pleasantly with our hosts and other trekkers while enjoying a hot meal and cold drinks, was a welcome break from the arduous hiking and monotonous trail food. The congeniality of these picnics reminded me of other happy picnics.

Picnic

Let us cross over the river
where we can spread our blankets
and rest under the shade of the trees
while we enjoy our picnic.

Hold on, kids, don't run off just yet.
    Everybody has to carry something.
        and help set up.

    Let me carry that basket.
Here, you take the chips and run,
get us a table, if there still is one.

Who wants some chocolate?
Promise not to eat all of it?
        Hmmm. I do like the taste of chocolate.

I think we're all set now.
You kids can go play,
but don't wander,
    it won't be long until dinner.

        Has anyone seen the net?
Must be in the car.
    Here take my keys.
    Don't forget to bring them back to me.

Anyone want a beer?
        We've got something stronger for later.
Will you open the wine for us, dear?

    Let's go start up the grill.
        Relax, have a seat. I'll man the grill.
All right, I'll supervise for a while.

        Could I have a hit of that cigarette?

(Cough) I never could get the hang of it,
but I do like the smell of cigarette.

Are you smoking, honey?
No, not really. Just keeping bugs away.
You promised not to do that anymore.
I know.

I'm hungry. Is anything ready yet?
We have some chicken, hot dogs, and
burgers.
Go ahead, you can eat, I'll take over.

Did you leave room for dessert?
Did you bring your
chocolate chip cookies?
Here they are.
We have pie and sherbet.

I sure could use a cup of coffee.
We do have coffee and ... ta da, a pot!
I love the smell of coffee brewing.

Who wants to play catch?
We brought cards and games for later.
Good, I've been itching for a rematch.

It's starting to get dark.
And buggy.
Back to school.
And work tomorrow.
So much to do and over so quickly.

Did you have a good time, dear?
I cannot think of a better way
to spend such a beautiful day.

Water was always welcome Trail Magic. Stopping to filter or purify water became tedious. In 2013, I carried too much water, walking into camp carrying two or three liters, four to six pounds of excess weight that I had carried all day. In 2014, I carried too little water and spent one parched night miles from water. I ran short on several hot days with long distances between

FOLLOW THE BLAZE:
A PATH LINED BY
VIRGINIA BLUEBELLS,
VIRGINIA

springs and decided to ask for water from day-hikers. My ability to manage water remains under development.

My first experience with Trail Magic was on my first day at the Visitor Center back at Amicalola State Park in Georgia. Technically, I'm not even sure I can claim to have started my trek at that point. I was standing outside the restroom when a hiking instructor promised his group would top off my water when I met them returning from Springer. Just as I was contemplating a walk down a side trail to fetch water, they arrived and filled my containers. It was exactly what I needed.

On my second day, I had accepted the trail name "Apa" with great emotion, so much so that I committed the first of many mistakes. I walked past the last small stream (more a trickle than a stream) before reaching my destination for the night. Realizing my mistake, I walked back to get water. When I arrived at the campground later, a local day-hiker had left four gallon jugs of water there. The extra distance had been unnecessary if only I had dared to trust his earlier promise to leave water by the road.

Of course, you couldn't rely on Trail Magic to appear. Even when it did appear, Trail Magic operated on the principle of first come, first served. Anyone passing by could help themselves to the water. I couldn't expect there to be any of it by the time I arrived, especially because I was slow. At first, I

Thus in recompense for a ride through green Virginia on a bright April morning in 2014 back to the Trail at Jenning Creek, Virginia, I wrote "Emeralds" for a young girl.

was always missing Trail Magic because I arrived late, after it had run out or the Trail Angels had packed up and left. I had to hike back to get water for myself just in case it was gone when I arrived.

Even labeling Trail Magic didn't guarantee its delivery to the intended recipient. Once a family left a cooler of Trail Magic for a friend coming up the Trail. It was high-quality, too: candy, protein bars, soda, sugary Danish, fruit, and much more, even small bottles of whiskey and vodka. They labeled the cooler with his trail name. For everyone else, they explained that they had hung a bag of goodies from a nearby tree. I took a couple of candy bars for Up Hill and myself. When I met the trekker later, I asked him about his wonderful Trail Magic. He said he never got any of it—not a single piece. Everyone, not just through-hikers, will help themselves to just "a little," until there is almost nothing remaining and at that point, others think, "He must have taken what he wanted and left this for us." Sometimes a group out for a weekend unknowingly will descend on Trail Magic, vultures consuming it all, leaving nothing for anyone else. Thus the first rule of Trail Magic is to enjoy it when it is available, provided it was not intended for another.

I became superstitious about declining Trail Magic. Every time I turned it down, saying I didn't need it, I came to regret that decision.

My best day for Trail Magic happened right before Bland, Virginia. An embankment along a dirt road invited me to put my pack down, take a seat, lean back, and tilt my hat over my eyes. I was going to rest and power nap. Soon I heard a car stop in front of me. I lifted the brim of my hat. "Are you a through-hiker?" a lady asked through a rolled-down window. "Yes," I said, wondering what else she thought I might be. "Well, we just went shopping, what do you need?" They fixed a sandwich, then gave me soda, candy, and snacks to take with me.

After they left, my energy had been restored so I got my gear together and started down the road. Another car pulled alongside. "Are you a through-hiker?" they asked. That second Trail Angel was the through-hiker who had broken his leg in Maine just short of completing his through-hike. Now he and his wife come out every year to support other hikers.

There was no way to repay Trail Magic, and there was no expectation of payment, only gratitude, conversation, and geniality. Sometimes I expressed my gratitude by offering to recite one of my poems.

A few times someone asked me to write a poem about them. Since I didn't know the person well, I promised only to try. Once, however, a mother asked me to write a poem for her daughter. Thus in recompense for a ride through green Virginia on a bright April morning in 2014 back to the Trail at Jenning Creek, Virginia, I wrote "Emeralds" for a young girl. This is for you, Mary Katherine.

Emeralds
Once, I rode an emerald mile
with a mother and her daughter.
When the young girl turned to smile,
I swear I saw emeralds
sparkle in her eyes.

FIRST AMONG TRAIL ANGELS

The overwhelming majority of hikers on the Appalachian Trail were honest and supportive of each other. There were many acts of kindness among through-hikers: sharing food, patching gear, treating cuts, wounds, and blisters. At the end of a long day in 2013, Danno gave me a can of soda he had carried. I shared first aid supplies to those in need and other items they wanted. HoBo lanced and bandaged a painful blister for me. While I seem to be among those unaffected by poison ivy, Candy Pants treated a rash on my arm caused by a series of scratches from a bush. A former EMT treated a cut on Danno's hand. Everyone helped each other. Trekkers themselves rank first among Trail Angels.

One selfless incident affected me greatly. At Muskrat Shelter in a bad snowstorm, a trekker made hot tea for everyone until his fuel ran out. With his dark beard and long hair, he resembled portraits of Jesus, but he declined that name. Before I fell asleep on that bitter night, I contemplated the young man's generosity.

Ermino's Prayer
In faith fervently,
I pray to you, my lord and deity,
to grant this litany:

to my friends and family,
continued health and safety;
to those who serve,

protection from enemies;
to those who suffer,
respite from their misery;
to the poor,
relief from poverty;
to those who prosper,
compassion and humility;
to all of us,
gratitude and clemency
and as we are able,
generosity.

My friend Slim had provided me with the ultimate Trail Magic when he invited me to his home. Then in 2014 Cruise and Corn Dog matched Slim's generosity by surprising me with a reservation at a bed and breakfast including two days of slack-packing. We haggled over their paying for this, ultimately settling on a 50-50 split. When I went to pay, however, the manager said everything had been taken care of and she was under orders not to accept any of my money. How do I say thanks for that? How do I pay them back? My daughters gave me an idea for something that I am pursuing: an artist's rendition of a photo taken on the Trail.

Trail Magic lifted my spirits, not just the food, rides, or supplies, but because it felt good to know that there were people thinking about us and caring about our condition, that they had empathy and compassion for us. In the end, though, my trail friends were the best Trail Magic. Unfortunately, not everyone could be trusted.

BAD BEHAVIOR ON THE TRAIL

Almost all trekkers were kind, helpful, and supportive. A few, however, behaved badly. Theft rarely occurred among the hikers. One reason it didn't happen more often was that no one wanted to carry anything extra. There was a joke told in various forms, for instance, "You could leave your wallet, a canister of fuel, and a candy bar on a table and when you came back, only the candy bar would be gone."

The joke was the truth. Once when I was rushing to catch a shuttle, I left my camera on a table at a hostel. When I returned several hours later, my camera was still there despite the dozens of people coming and going.

Yet, theft did occur. One time a pair of shorts, a belt, and a water bottle disappeared overnight. There were few present, thus a likely culprit was quickly identified. Some young bucks took off after him. I don't know if they caught him or what happened.

I never felt in danger from any hikers, although sometimes I moved on rather than spend the night near
someone who made me feel uneasy.

Only one instance of a disagreement between trekkers escalated. A young man was upset at the noise made by a group. During the night, he poured instant mashed potatoes over the tent and gear of an innocent party. In the morning, everything of theirs was covered in goo. He was a fast hiker and had left early to get far ahead of them.

I never felt in danger from any hikers, although sometimes I moved on rather than spend the night near someone who made me feel uneasy. I trusted my instincts. One night, I stopped early upon learning that a home-less man was living with his dog at the shelter ahead. In another instance, a young couple appeared to be hiding from the police because the pair questioned me extensively about the activities of the authorities at a nearby parking lot. One man turned himself into the police. He was tired of hiding out. Another time, security from several federal agencies removed one troubled young man from the Trail on federal land. Corn Dog said the man had threatened a park employee. Hikers had been alarmed by his strange behavior, and the park employee had gone to talk with him. Authorities kept their eyes on the Trail.

Once I was suspicious of three young locals who hurried past me. Back at the roadside, they had invited me to drink moonshine with them, but I just waved and moved on. Now, they were waiting ahead, grinning at me as I approached. *What were they up to?* Two were standing to one side of the trail with the third crouching on the other side. When I passed between them, they could easily trip me or push me over. A trekker carries more than a thousand dollars' worth of gear, plus cash, credit cards and bank cards. You have to be careful about whom you trust.

I was walking with my trekking poles shortened, one in each hand hori-zontally. In college, I had chosen fencing for physical education. I'm no rival of D'Artagnan of the Three Musketeers, but I can stab, and there is a spike at the end of each pole that would leave a nasty hole in someone's flesh. When I got close to the young men, I darted behind the one crouching, causing him to jump up and turn toward me with an expression of surprise and fear. When I looked back to see if they were following, they were standing and watching me. If they had been planning anything, my movement caused them to reconsider. I tipped my hat with my pole then proceeded without incident. We met up atop the Bald where they sat among a crowd; they seemed to be decent fellows. We spoke briefly, and they offered some moonshine as a reward for reaching the top. I declined again but thanked them.

AN AGENDA

Triveni and I had been together longer than any of my relationships since my marriage ended. We had talked about what we wanted in our remaining years. We both wanted to travel around the country. We shared our lists of places we wanted to go. I had enjoyed hiking and camping so much that first summer, I suggested we drive to Alaska the next year. I had always wanted to visit Alaska, as had she. Why not now, together? We had called our previous trips, our "Great Adventures." Alaska would be another Great Adventure for us.

She proposed we purchase a trailer so we could pursue our dreams of traveling around the country over the coming years. I sold my sports car and bought a pick-up truck. I insisted on a travel trailer with its own bathroom. I joked that a lighter pop-up or fold-out camper would be like setting a buffet out for the bears. In fact, some parks do not allow pop-out and fold-out trailers due to the danger from bears attracted by the food inside.

In some ways, all road trips must be alike. There is the planning and preparation, delays in getting started, the exhilaration of finally getting underway, and the long drive itself: inside, conversation, car games, snacks, naps, music, and books; outside, cities, towns, scenery, and traffic, plus getting to know each other better and finding out exactly how much we could stand to be with each other confined in a small place for long hours over several days.

Preparing for a drive to Alaska resembled planning for my later hike on the Appalachian Trail. Due to limitations on weight and space, we couldn't bring everything we wanted. We would be gone a long time, traveling great distances. We had to plan where to fuel up and resupply, select where to spend the night and identify side trips to places we wanted to visit, knowing we might never be there again. The differences were that we would be driving, not walking; we would have all the luxuries and conveniences of home without having to carry them on our backs.

During the fall and winter of 2010, both Triveni and I were busy with work, family, and other activities as well as the arrangements that we needed to complete before starting our long journey away from house and families. After a year back in the real world, we began to look forward to getting away on our next Great Adventure and to spending more time together. At last, the summer of 2011 arrived.

I can still remember how excited Triveni and I were to leave for Alaska. Just hitting the road can be exhilarating, but this was going to be a road trip to beat all other road trips. It would be our Greatest Adventure yet.

Finally, everything was taken care of and we were ready to go. It was the day of our departure.

On Our Way
Locking the front door,
climbing into the truck,
keys in the purse, purse on the floor,
no turning back now, wish us good luck.

At last, we're on our way.
Where this road goes and how it ends,
we don't know and we don't care
because, at last, we're going somewhere.

Sometimes we'll laugh, sometimes not.
We may sing, talk or be quiet.
We might get cold, wet, or hot
And, who knows, this may be all we'll ever get.

So enjoy this day
because the miles may be long
but the journey will be quick.
Today we're healthy and strong

and we're going somewhere.
Where this road goes and how it ends,
we don't know and we shouldn't care
because, at least, we're going somewhere.

To reach Alaska, we would drive the Alaskan-Canadian Highway (AL-CAN), which had been constructed during World War II by the U.S. Corp of Engineers in order to deliver supplies needed by troops in Alaska. Our plan included dashing across the Midwest and plains of the United States and Canada, into the Rockies and the start of the ALCAN at Dawson Creek, British Columbia, about 2,250 miles in four days, an eminently doable distance. This first leg of our journey would be about the equivalent of driving from the Midwest to the West, a drive that truckers and others accomplish all of the time.

We quickly discovered it was one thing to plan what we could do in a day, several days, or a week, but it was another thing to accomplish it. In order to have as much time in Alaska as possible, we pushed ourselves, driving long hours to arrive as quickly as we could at the beginning of the ALCAN at Dawson Creek. While we were relentless, pulling a trailer slowed us and the road seemed, at times, to be endless. Everything we did took longer than we had planned. We drove more miles than we expected; by the end of the trip, an additional 10 percent above our estimate. We ran into more construction than we expected, and flooding that year caused us to detour. We always seemed to spend more time on the little things: fueling up, resupplying, having lunch, checking in, setting up and tearing down, and so forth. Our days were longer than we anticipated, and we rested less.

We climbed the palm of Michigan, crossed the bridge at the Mackinaw Straits then west across the Upper Peninsula of Michigan along the shores of Lake Superior before camping at a pristine campground by a lake in Wisconsin. In the morning we entered Minnesota to the unexpected beauty of Duluth Bay. While crossing Minnesota, I was amused to see the many signs proclaiming the start of the Mississippi River, as if any branch, leaf, or root could claim title to the beginning of a tree. Didn't they all equally deserve a sign? When we left the forests of eastern Minnesota, we entered wet farmland. Warned by truckers about long waits and roads that had been closed, we chose to avoid the flooding in North Dakota by crossing into Canada and camping south of Winnipeg, Manitoba. Instead of heading west to Calgary, we took the scenic Yellowhead Highway northwest directly toward Edmonton, Alberta. We stopped for the night at Battleford, Saskatchewan, before rushing through Edmonton, eager to reach Dawson Creek and the beginning of the ALCAN. In four days, we had driven over two thousand miles and were more than half way to the Alaskan border.

A few memories dominate my recollection of our mad dash to Dawson Creek. The sensation of driving is foremost. Sometimes on a long drive across states or cross country now, I feel like I'm on that journey once again.

The Road to Calgary

I dream of an open highway
along the shores of an inland sea,
of hillside houses above a harbor
hidden in a deep water bay.

I drive through wetted woods,
on a road lined by Northern trees,
across sodden marshes and overflowing streams,
labeled Mississippi.

I come out among flooded fields,
now dark blue, shallow seas,
where utility poles rise like masts
marking fortunes sunken below;

followed by flowered fields
of canola bean,
more yellow than I'd ever seen
or will until I pass this way again.

I pass through narrow towns stretched thin
by a taut line running quickly
toward the horizon,
drawn by dreams Alaskan.
(continued)

To help pass the time, we listened to music and books. It's easy to be inspired by significant events and great places, but for me, the sweetest inspiration comes from the smallest parts of life, such as a random song on the radio prompting the question, "Who is that?"

Just a Song

It's just a song on the radio
by someone whose name I've forgotten
If ever I cared to learn,

a song in a familiar pattern,
old but for the singing and playing,
of love and loss we all know.

They sing so sadly of sorrow,
how badly their heart must have been broken.
Such emotion must be earned;

something tragic to make their heart burn
rendering their singing like pale smoke trailing
from a fire dying below.

Does singing relieve them of their woe,
finally purged and forgotten,
no longer of thought or concern?

Or being too proud and stubborn,
neither forgiving nor forgetting,
still keeping a bitter ember aglow

and their singing grand bravado?
Or upon restoration has this precious heart
become a treasured urn,

waiting for a faithful visitor to return,
remembering and their memories creating
this melancholy nocturne?

	Estimated Milage
Dawson Creek, British Columbia	
Liard River Hot springs Provincial Park, British Columbia	2798
Whitehorse, Yukon	3207
Alaska Border	3506
Tok, Alaska	3634
Copper Center, Alaska	3742
McCarthy, Alaska	
Seward, Alaska	4081
Homer, Alaska	4250
Anchorage, Alaska	4472
Denali National Park	4712
Fairbanks, Alaska	4835
Chena Hot Springs, Alaska	
Haines , Alaska	5554
Skagway, Alaska	5554
Chilcoot Trail	
Hider, Alaska	6252
Jasper, Alberta	6921
Banff, Alberta	7101
Calgary, British Columbia	7180
Michigan	9077
Actual mileage	10542

It was as if the world had been stretched outward and upward.

Once Triveni and I started the ALCAN, we slowed down, stopping more often and for longer periods. My insistence at staying on our schedule for reaching Dawson Creek—I am obsessive about keeping to a plan, a trait that would hurt me on the Appalachian Trail—had come at a price: we were both exhausted. Also, while the ALCAN roadway was surprisingly good, we had to drive more slowly because of the frost heaves. When water freezes under a road, it raises the roadbed. Frost heaves resemble the tail end of a roller coaster ride with undulating waves of ups and downs. Hitting a wave or a series of these waves at high speed risks doing serious damage to a vehicle and trailer, such as breaking axles and springs. Contents of the trailer would be strewn about. Even worse, appliances, such as the fridge, stove, or microwave might break free.

Fortunately frost heaves were easy to spot, especially once we learned to watch for drunken trees off the roadway. Due to the shallow thawed soil in areas of permafrost, tree roots are unable to penetrate the soil deeply enough to support the trees sturdily. A frost heave lifts the trees, which tilt and fall every which way, resembling a crowd of drunks stumbling about. When we saw a stand of drunken and fallen trees, we quickly slowed down. Sill, we hit a couple at high speed, thankfully to no consequence, except to rattle our nerves and pop open some of the cabinets, allowing items to escape.

During our drive through the dry American West in the lower 48 states, every turn had brought another amazing view. Due to its aridness and thin, sparse vegetation, the impression was one of veiled beauty.

In contrast, my strongest impression of Northwest Canada and Alaska was created by its immense scale and remoteness. It was as if the world had been stretched outward and upward. Everything seemed to have been enlarged, including the distances between destinations, which were much greater than in the lower 48. We slowly approached mountain ranges. We drove through green landscapes hour after hour. We saw other vehicles, but there were many places, where if a tire blew out or we lost control and drove off the road into the bush, no one might ever know. It felt like we more alone than I had ever felt before.

Much of the region was so remote, sometimes we spotted wreckage from a traffic accident pushed off to the side of the road and abandoned. We saw the remains of one trailer plastered against a hillside. The valuable metal and mechanical parts had been stripped, leaving just the scattered debris.

Whitehorse was exactly what we needed after driving for those long hours. Anyone driving to Alaska would be glad to spend a day or two there.

Driving

Driving to Alaska may sound exciting,
and there are rivers, lakes, mountains, and glaciers,
plus the wildlife, fishing, camping, and hiking,
But it's five hundred gallons of gasoline
and five thousand miles, so it's mostly driving.
You will quickly settle into a routine.
Some like to sleep in with afternoon driving,
staying up late on their phone and computer
or joining the partiers, talking and drinking
through the long daylight until almost morning,
but I prefer to spend the morning driving,
getting up and out, loaded up on caffeine,
stopping in the afternoon then relaxing.
But no matter how you cut it and vary it,
It's still eleven eight-hour days of driving
just to get there and another eleven
five-hundred-mile days to get back.
It's a long way to Alaska and it's all driving.

Except you can't drive like that, nor should you try.
So you take short days, rest days, and sanity days
camping by a river, lake, mountain, or glacier
to see the wildlife, go fishing or hiking
but sooner or later you're back to driving,
because it's a long way to Alaska and it's all driving,
driving, driving, driving, and then more driving.

It must sound to you like I'm complaining
but I'm not, because it was amazing
and nothing I had ever done could compare.
I wouldn't have skipped a mile if I could've.

A NICE PLACE
TO PICNIC:
STRAWBERRY FLATS,
MUNCHO LAKE,
BRITISH COLUMBIA,
MILEPOST 438

Even now I sometimes find myself dreaming
I'm driving that long road or remembering
moments of breathtaking beauty,
of idyllic picnics by inspiring scenery,
and an overwhelming sensation of living.

Still it's a long time to spend driving,
because it is a long way to Alaska and it's all driving
but I wouldn't take back a second of that driving,
driving, driving, and still more driving, even if I could.

One of the nicest aspects of the drive to Alaska was stopping at the hot springs along the way. The first springs, Liard Hot Springs in British Columbia, were located at milepost 478. With the right timing, it was possible to arrive early, enjoy the springs before they became crowded, leave for lunch, then return to the springs in the afternoon, have dinner, and return once again in the evening.

When we arrived at the city of Whitehorse, milepost 887, in the Northwest Territory, we had driven more than 3,200 miles without stopping in a city or town other than to gas up, grab a meal, and resupply. At this point, we were eager for a taste of civilization.

Red Dress, Blue Dress

Put on your red dress.
Put on your blue dress.
Wear a ribbon
in your hair.
Red dress, blue dress,
ribbon in your hair,

Put on a dress shirt.
Put on your new tie.
Trim your beard and
brush your hair.
Dress shirt, new tie,
brush your hair,

I don't care,
what you wear.

Put on your lipstick.
Put on your makeup.
Wear your fancy underwear.
Red dress, blue dress,
ribbon in your hair,
lipstick, makeup,
fancy underwear,

Put on your sport coat.
Put on your dress shoes.
Try to be all debonair.
Dress shirt, new tie,
brush your hair,
sport coat, dress shoes,
debonair.

I don't care,
what you wear.
I love you,
you love me,
how happy will we be

when you wear your green dress,
when your wear your yellow dress,
when you put a ribbon in your hair,

when you wear a white shirt,
when you wear a brand new tie,
when you run a brush through
your hair.

when you wear your lipstick,
when you wear your makeup,
when you put on those underwear?

when you wear your sport coat,
when you wear your dress shoes,
when you act all debonair?

I love you,
you love me,
how happy will we be?

Red dress, blue dress,
ribbon in your hair,
will I care
what you wear,

Dress shirt, new tie,
brush your hair,

when I see those underwear?

when you act all debonair?

I love you,
you love me,
how happy will we be

when you wear a white dress,   *when your wear a white shirt,*
when you carry flowers,   *when you wear a bow tie,*
when your wear something blue, *when you wear a fancy suit,*
when you carry something borrowed, *when your wear a boutonniere,*
when you put a ribbon   *when you shave your beard*
in your hair?   *and trim your hair?*

Due to the nearby gold and oil fields, Whitehorse was a lively, booming town, a real town with large stores, a downtown, good restaurants, and a brewery. We stayed at the hot springs where we relaxed and warmed ourselves. Whitehorse was exactly what we needed after driving for those long hours. Anyone driving to Alaska would be glad to spend a day or two there.

From Whitehorse, it was a couple more days into Alaska. We stopped at the international border for pictures before spending the night near Tok, the first crossroads in Alaska. Instead of completing the ALCAN, we turned south toward Wrangell-St. Elias National Park, the largest national park in the United States.

THE WRANGELL MOUNTAINS, NEAR THE BORDER OF THE UNITED STATES AND CANADA

THE LOWER
KENNICOTT GLACIER
IS DISGUISED AS
HUGE MOUNDS
OF DIRT.

We left the truck and trailer at a campground near Wrangell-St. Elias and took a shuttle to McCarthy, where we stayed several nights. From McCarthy, another shuttle took us up to the historic Kennecott mill and we hiked from there. One day we walked out onto the Kennicott glacier. In the past, the glacier had covered the valley to such depth that no one knew a valley actually lay underneath. The glacier has been retreating since the 1800s. I suspect people just never wondered what was under the glacier.

Although the glacier appeared small, the visible ice is only the upper portion of the glacier. The lower, larger portion is covered by dust and dirt, which absorbs the sun's rays, melting the ice underneath and making the lower part of the glacier too dangerous to walk on.

Another day we hiked the trail up to the Bonanza mine, 4.5 miles one-way and 3,800 feet of elevation gain. Again, I had problems with the rapid change in altitude. I rested but every time I tried to go higher, I got dizzy. The only cure for altitude sickness is to go to a lower elevation, where the air is denser. After several attempts, I gave up. The thought of losing my balance and rolling down the mountainside stopped me.

From Wrangell-St. Elias National Park, we next made our way toward Seward on the Kenai Peninsula, where we parked at the end of the road by the bay. Resurrection Bay was an exceptionally calm, beautiful, sheltered bay. I rose early one morning to take pictures of the bay in the dim light. To the left, at the head of the bay, were the lights of the city; across the bay a few house lights at the base of the mountains that were outlined against the night sky; in front of me, anchored boats waiting and to my right, the entrance to the bay.

Resurrection Bay

As I sit down by the bay
watching the children at play,
gentle waves carry my thoughts
to another time, another place.
It seems so far and long ago.

We were young and, oh, so free.
No responsibility held us,
filling our days with endless chores,
leaving our life and love
but a trace and a shadow.

We used to walk hand in hand
around town and among the market stands,
stop to dine and chat the day away,
find some music and join the crowd to dance
with its ebb and flow,

Then rest down by the sea
where your hair would envelop me,
your curls crashing upon my chest and face
until a tide seized us in tight embrace
and then release.

Are our days lost forever,
swept away by an inevitable tide,
or do they yet struggle to escape
from beneath the flood
of daily necessities?

Sometimes when I see you stare I wonder:
is it I or some other lover
with whom you dance outside your window?

Forgive me, dear, while I disturb your reverie
and interrupt your memories,
but please take my hand and dance with me
once again in reality.

RESURRECTION BAY,
SEWARD, ALASKA

After Seward we drove to Homer, from which we could fly across the inlet to Katmai National Park where we could see bears. As our plane approached landing, we grew excited at seeing solitary bears on the little streams below us. The plane landed on a small lake. We walked about a mile to sit by a large stream and suddenly we were surrounded by bears. At one point, I counted 30, but kept losing count because they moved in and out of view. We had been told to stay seated and not to move so as to not alarm the bears. We hardly spoke; it was like we were in church. For a while, we watched three bears playing with remarkably gentle ferocity, swatting, wrestling, and leaping upon each other. Any of their acts of play would have crushed, decapitated, or gutted us. With no firearms or bear spray allowed on the plane, we were protected only by the experience of our guides and the stream, full of salmon easy for the bears to catch.

Sitting by that stream watching the bears feast upon the salmon, I pondered, *which would I rather be: a bear or a salmon?* It was not as easy a question to answer as one might think. Outside Homer, we had seen an eagle nesting. Kayaking across Resurrection Bay, we had come across the desiccated carcass of an eagle. At Denali, we would see wolves eating a caribou they had killed and then a bear taking his share after chasing the wolves away. I contemplated the life of the bears around me whose survival depends on what they can find, catch, or steal, whether they are the young and fit bears at this river brimming with fish or are instead the old and infirm bears by desolate streams.

To be a Bear

When the salmon run,
filling the streams with their sweet red meat,
the skin and brains rich in fat,
but best of all roe to eat,
then I would be a bear,
finding my place by a stream
by threat and combat,
yet yielding to higher rank.
There to watch and wait, pounce, and splash,
diving to catch a silver flash.
Savoring its taste in my mouth,
I would carry my prize to a nearby bank,
where standing proud watch, constantly aware
of those who might try to steal my catch,
I crush the skull, strip the skin, and feast.

Or when the caribou calve
filling the land with young to have,
tender meat to stalk, chase, catch, and kill,
then I would be a wolf,
quickly tearing the fur and eating my fill,
much better than the rest of the year,
when we make do with unaesthetic
injured, scraggly, old, and sick.

Or in summer's warm updraft,
rising smoothly into the atmosphere,
where like a cloud I waft
and from those regal heights, lord of the sky,
I survey the land and sea
free from snow and ice cover,
judging spring's and summer's supply
of prey in plenty,
then I would be a raptor
quickly turn, dive, and take a hare.

But not an ancient predator
facing another winter slowdown,
searching for anything to eat:
a carcass, a scrap, or shrew,
to feel myself weakening,
chasing but failing to catch,

straining but unable to climb,
beating my wings too weak to fly,
dying a long, slow death,
starving until lying down,
spending my last energy
straining to rise one last time,
but spent and out of breath,
I lie down, carrion
for some other desperate beast.

And not a caribou who stand and chew
like cattle fattening in their pen
waiting for the butcher
to begin the slaughter,
fleeing and escaping this day
but to be caught another day.

I wonder what drives the salmon so.
Is it only instinct that makes them run
or do they hear death calling, "come"?
Could they know of the gauntlet that waits,
hasten to meet a bite or slash
and die in a momentary flash
or do they run to beat those teeth and claws
and have one last taste of victory?
If so, then I would be a salmon,
join their run and share their fate.

But not to die as a bear,
sneaking into my den,
sleeping and starving there,
never waking, disappear.

If you wonder why I continue to pursue adventure or search for love and romance at my advancing age, the answer is that I would rather spend my remaining years as a salmon running than withdraw peacefully like an old bear. There will be peace enough in the care of others.

MOTHER WATCHING ME, NORTH OF PORTERS FIELD BEFORE SPY ROCK, VIRGINIA

CHAPTER 6: *Normalcy*

A last habit
like old folks feeling frail
avoiding risk,
forgoing excitement,
settling for familiarity
and contentment.

A ROUTINE

By 2014, I had become comfortable on the Trail. It remained difficult, but I was making fewer mistakes and almost never got into a complicated situation any more. The Trail had become my home and, when not on it, I was thinking of the Trail and preparing to return: purchasing supplies, repairing and replacing gear, dropping some items and adding others and making plans. Almost every night, I dreamt or remembered a place, an event, or someone.

I must have become a quieter hiker, because I sometimes startled people by walking up on them. When I stopped to rest on a convenient rock or fallen tree, a bird might land next to me, or a squirrel or chipmunk walk in front or around me. Sometimes they would stop to look at me, chewing on a morsel while keeping an eye on me, then move on. Even deer approached me quizzically. *What were they thinking?* I wondered. Were they trying to identify this misshapen beast of burden? Were they assessing my intentions or, perhaps, only begging? If I moved at all, even just an eye, they turned and bounded away through the woods. But if I stayed still, they remained nearby.

WILDLIFE ON THE AT

The more a hiker hurries, the less opportunity they have to experience nature; whereas the more they stop to enjoy, the fewer miles they cover. Ultimately every trekker has to decide on the proper balance between distance, speed, time, stopping to enjoy nature and the approaching winter deadline at Katahdin.

In 2014, south of Spy Rock, Virginia, I spied a mother black bear and large cub, probably a yearling, ahead of me on the trail. At my approach, the mother left the cub by the trail, scrounging around at something, while

I yelled, "Hey bear!"—it was what we did in Alaska—and banged my hiking poles, but the bears didn't move.

she hid behind the brush. I could see her peering out at me. Her body was completely hidden. She might have been waiting to ambush me. I wasn't comfortable turning around in order to go down the rise I had just ascended. I just stood there, waiting for them to move.

I snapped a picture without trying to focus the camera. Even with the image enlarged, I can barely make out the mother's face peering through the brush. People have been mauled, even killed by bears while they took pictures of the bear charging toward them. A hiker died in late 2014 taking pictures of a bear in New Jersey. Some speculate that a raised camera hides a hiker's face so the bear thinks the hiker isn't paying attention or maybe raising one's hands and arms resembles lifting a rifle, thereby threatening the bear. I only knew not to take my eyes off the mother peering at me from her hiding place. I had the uneasy feeling that she was ready, if not eager, for a fight.

I yelled, "Hey bear!"—it was what we did in Alaska—and banged my hiking poles, but the bears didn't move. So, in a stand-off, we waited. At first, I was afraid to move, concerned my movement be interpreted as a threat or as fear. Gradually I began to feel that she did not perceive me as a threat. Finally impatient, I took one step off to the side of the trail away from them and paused. At that, the mother moved in the other direction with the cub following. I cautiously made my way forward while they disappeared downhill on the other side of the trail. Had she been waiting to see which direction I took? Who knows the mind of a bear?

In Shenandoah National Park, I surprised a bear defecating on the trail. He quickly ran off, as if embarrassed to be caught in the act. There was a lot of bear scat on the Trail, and sometimes it was still moist and warm with steam rising. When I saw small droppings, I knew a cub was around and I became alert. One night, my friend Otto, Danno's first companion, and a young man from Michigan were hiking north when they met two bears on the Trail going south. It was a tense standoff until the Michigan man made a racket and the bears ran off.

My closest encounter with a bear came in Connecticut in 2013. I had spent a rainy night in a shelter with a young man and his dog. We knew many people in common. He updated me on their whereabouts and condition and we shared stories about them into the evening. In the middle of the night, the dog suddenly jumped into the shelter by me, then settled in between me and his owner. In the morning, another young man came into camp. They left together. While I was putting on my pack, I sensed something behind me. I turned to see a large male bear much closer than I liked. He was a big boy and I was trapped in the shelter. As soon as I saw him, he took off through the woods. I'd say "to my relief," except that I hadn't time to feel threatened. It was over that quickly.

The bear had been coming into camp to look for leftovers. People sometimes left bags of Trail Magic in the shelters. Hikers left food in the shelters they no longer wanted or needed. Animals learned to check the shelters when people moved off.

Why had the bear come into camp while I was there? The bear might have been waiting for the dog to leave. Or, the bear knew that two of us had spent the night in the shelter and seeing two hikers leave in the morning, he felt it was safe to enter the camp. Apparently bears can count, at least, to two.

Outside the national parks (where hunting is prohibited), bear sightings were uncommon. All the friendly and unwary bears have been shot, and the cubs are taught to avoid us. In my four months on the Trail, I saw six, most of those in the Shenandoah National Park (where they were not hunted). In 2013, ironically, Candy Pants, who was terrified of bears, seemed to be seeing more bears than anyone.

We saw so few bears, it was easy to forget that they were out there. We got lazy. Instead of hanging our food from a tree, we hung it in the shelter. Some people started to keep their food bags in their tents. Some hikers even used their food bag for a pillow. I did that on some nights until hearing that a bear ripped open the tent of an acquaintance, grabbed his food bag, and took off into the woods with it. Mercifully, the bear did not touch him. I am more careful now, even though others might tease me for being cautious.

Once I saw Danno leap into the air. *What was he doing?* I wondered. Slim was laughing; Danno looked agitated. A highly experienced hiker, not much got to Danno, but this time, a snake had shot across the Trail between Danno's legs.

In Pennsylvania, I heard many snakes moving away through the leaf litter. I gave the rattlesnakes plenty of space, although one did rear up when I moved around it. The nonpoisonous black snakes rattled the dry leaves with the hard tip of their tail, making a sound that imitates the warning of a rattlesnake. Hurrying toward Duncannon, Pennsylvania, anticipating town food, soda, and beer, I heard a rattle close by my left heel. If there is an event called the walking broad jump, I set the record that day. When I turned to look back, I couldn't see anything. As soon as my eyes focused on the black snake, it shot off into the woods. I was shocked by its speed. If he had

charged toward me, I'm not certain I could have leaped away. Thankfully, snakes do not charge, but ambush. In 2014, one unfortunate hiker was bitten by a black snake as he stepped over a log.

With warm weather, insects emerged, creepy-crawly things that I could see outside my net tent, as well as bees and other flying insects. I've always had a fondness for bees, despite having been stung multiple times, perhaps because they are among the first harbingers of spring heralding the arrival of flowers.

Oh, to be a Bee
Oh, to be a bee
and bumble about a tree,
but the bumble does not bee
in a tree
but in a humble hole beneath the tree
does the bumble bee.

However, I did not appreciate the ticks, mosquitos, and flies. Lyme disease may be the most well-known of the tick-borne diseases, but researchers continue to find more. As recently as 2013, scientists discovered a previously unknown disease suspected to be infecting as many as 250,000 people in New York and surrounding states. In early 2015, a man died from a previously unknown tick-borne disease.

Despite all that we know about ticks, some hikers were not prepared for them. In Pennsylvania, there was a meadow called "the Tick Field," near the Superfund site after Lehigh Gap. One young man claimed to have picked 80 ticks off himself after he passed through it. I don't think he was exaggerating. I was happy I had soaked my shoes and boots, socks, and other clothes in permethrin, which repels and kills insects. When I crossed the Tick Field, I could see ticks jump off my boots. The only tick I ever discovered on me was when I was sitting at a picnic table next to a young man complaining about the ticks. When I felt something crawling on my leg, I looked down to see a tick crawling up my thigh. It served me right; I had been bragging about being tick-free. I moved away and stopped staying in shelters with others, choosing to camp if the shelter was occupied.

ACQUIESCENCE

The tenor of Triveni's and my trip to Alaska in 2011 differed from our previous trips out West the prior year. Instead of another Great Adventure, this trip seemed more like a tour. We drove long distances from one location to the next, where we would disembark to see an attraction or enjoy a few days before moving on. Something seemed to be missing from the experience.

When we left Homer, it had felt like we were headed home. In fact, we had completed only the first 4,500 miles of our trip. We had more than 6,000 miles to drive. Yet, we were tiring and it felt like the trip was winding down. Our inclination was transitioning from adventurous to the practical.

A Perfect Day
An elegant restaurant for a valentine,
music andante,
a table against a skyline,
a dance with a gentle sway,
a delicious dinner and a good wine;

A perfect end to a perfect day:
all it should have been
to hold my attention but my mind strayed
to a simpler inn
where we had gone to get away and see a play.

We had nothing but each other
but that was enough,
just spending our time together.
Now we have so much stuff
but are we any happier?

We took turns reading from a book of poems,
snacking on candy
and looking at pictures in an old album.
I drank my coffee
and you drank your tea laced with rum.

We stayed in our room all day, alone together,
perfectly lazy,
until we came out late for dinner
and had to hurry
through our meal to make it to the theater.

We remember that day with smiles and laughter
but not so back then.
Now we stay closer to the theater,
not to make that mistake again,
and we're never late for dinner.

From Homer, we made our way toward Denali National Park. We had learned to take advantage of good weather by staying in place longer in order to explore an area more completely. We relocated during bad weather, sometimes skipping places we had planned to stop. We gave up on doing everything we had planned; Alaska was too immense. You really could spend a lifetime there and not see it all.

In cloudy, rainy weather, the way to Denali was an uninspiring drive except that, once in view, the mountain never seemed to grow any larger. Only when we got up close could we appreciate its enormous dimensions. Of all the places we went in the state, no other place better represents Alaska. Denali is as massive as Alaska is vast.

It felt foolish waiting three days to get a clear view of Denali, but the mountain is so large that it makes its own weather. Consequently a clear view only happens about one day in three. Bus rides into the park relieved the boredom, but after Katmai, the wildlife seemed distant. The long drive in an old school bus rattling along a narrow, one-lane dirt road cut into cliffs was terrifyingly wonderful. There were pull-offs where buses could pass each other, with only inches of clearance. At times, we literally looked down cliffs at the wildlife below us. The driver seemed to know when to stop to give us the best views.

Denali is, in one way, the tallest mountain in the world. It rises from its base some 18,000 feet to its peak. No other mountain in the world has such a prominent profile. By comparison, Everest rises 13,000 feet from its surroundings.

We seemed somber with little to say to each other beyond, "Look at this, look at that." Was it boredom and exhaustion, or were we humbled by the presence of Denali? We struck up conversations with others, including a researcher from the United Kingdom. She was distraught at losing an expensive piece of equipment, most likely swept away in a river, perhaps after being investigated by a curious bear. We waited for a clear view of Denali.

I had seen the Rockies, I had seen the Alps, but I had seen nothing to rival Denali, alone in its singular magnificence.

On the third day, we saw Denali without clouds in the distance. By the time we got close, though, clouds were starting to form again. I had seen the Rockies, I had seen the Alps, but I had seen nothing to rival Denali, alone in its singular magnificence. White Denali dominated the low, dark surrounding hills and filled the horizon unlike any other mountain I had seen.

Standing before Denali, I thought about God again. After listening to all the arguments for and against the existence of God, until I could listen no more, I concluded that a person either believes in a God or in a universe that is god-like. Choose one or the other, and then the question becomes whether you should do something more than acknowledge, perhaps offer thanks, revere, or even worship.

I asked myself, if God exists, then from what did He make the universe? Did He create all of this from nothing? Or, did He use some other stuff just lying around—but then, from where had that stuff come: leftovers from another of His creations or created by another, greater god? If neither out of nothing nor from some undefined debris, had He created us from His own substance? Have we been created, if not by a word, as in the Bible, but by a divine breath? I did not have answers to these questions. If God is only a possibility, ought we not treat His world and each other, as His creations, with the respect due Him?

Before Denali

Standing before the great one, Denali
I understand why some might worship nature.
For Denali is much greater than you and me
and I can feel its massive weight pressing upon me.

But if awe is reason to worship a mountain
then what of the earth, sky, and ocean,
a god for this and every mountain
and others for the earth, sky, and ocean
and what of the wind, rain, stars, moon, and sun?
Why so many gods,
when one great god would subsume them all?

And if this one God is everything
and everything is this greatest God,
then how to explain you and me?
What is this persistent impression
of ourselves as distinct and unique
and not just fragile shards broken
by some eternal process
of mass wasting
from the singular certainty
that is this universe?

Is our life together an illusion,
a trick of evolution,
only a hesitation
while waiting to rejoin the whole
by an inverse process
of sedimentation,
when we lose our love and souls
as these pieces collapse into dust
to be recaptured by the universe
and our love vanished as if never?

Are we to disregard our essence,
our every thought and emotion
as devoid of any importance?
If our lives are to be discarded
as a masterful illusion,
I ask, "Who is being deluded
and who is the magician?"

⚜

If there is a God who wishes us to know Him, then our experience of His presence must be everywhere, from the great to the small and close at hand, within us, so that we may not overlook Him. Don't we all perceive ourselves as separate from the universe, distant, in some way, unique, valuable, and independent? We may be wrong, but if this impression is correct, then from where did the concept "I-am-in-this-world-but-not-of-it," come, but from a God who also must be separate from this universe? Perhaps it is self-importance, but for me the proof of God's existence comes from our perception that we have souls that we did not create. Or am I over-thinking and therefore mistaken?

From Denali we drove to Fairbanks to rest and resupply and then out to Chena Hot Springs. Of all the springs we visited, Chena was my favorite.

He seemed to enjoy charging the crowd, chasing us away in his innocence like we were seagulls fleeing a child running toward them on a beach.

The water ranged evenly in temperature from mildly warm to hot and very hot. The rocks beneath my feet were round and smooth. I slowly walked into and out of the hot zones, rubbing my feet back and forth across the rocks buffing them in a firm, gentle massage. My feet have never been happier.

We completed the ALCAN by traveling east to Delta Junction and then to Tok. In Canada, we turned south at Haines Junction, toward Haines. The drive to Haines was Alaska in miniature. The scenery and mountains were close, unlike the distant mountains and views we had experienced. We stopped by a lake for lunch and watched two swans resting on the water until they took flight.

THE GREAT ONE,
DENALI

This Swan

You are like a swan
resting on a quiet lake:
your arms folded alongside,
your head bent forward,
the curve of your neck and back,
your legs tucked under
lifting your behind,
the sun shining on our bed,
the sheets lightly folded
like ripples on a lake.

This swan turns her head,
to see me motionless behind her,
slowly turns away,
unfolds her wings
and with a single strong motion
lifts herself from our lake.
Her wings rowing back and forth,

sweeping the water
and world beneath her,
she holds to her place.

She passes in front of me
to admire her grace and beauty
before leaving our quiet lake,
to fly across the sea
to a place where people
recognize the purity
and peace of her soul
until returning
to our lake
to rest by me.

The Royal Canadian Mounted Police required every prospector to bring a list of supplies whose weight totaled more than one ton.

✦

We stayed at Haines for three days, enjoying the bears by the weir out-side of town. The bears knew the weir was an easy place for them to catch salmon. When a male cub came up to the road, we all scurried behind my truck, a ranger leading the way. She was concerned because this cub was showing no fear of humans. He seemed to enjoy charging the crowd, chasing us away in his innocence like we were seagulls fleeing a child running toward them on a beach.

A man foolishly left the roadway and walked out into bush to get closer to the mother bear and her cubs. Some people did not seem to respect wild-life. In Yellowstone, we had seen two young men stand between two bison to get a picture, turning their backs to one. They were within 20 feet of each animal. In Zion, a woman leaned toward a rattlesnake to get a better picture. If the disturbed animals were to charge at their human intruders, it could be a tragedy for both parties, because the animals would most likely have put down afterward.

CHILKOOT

From Haines, we took the ferry to Skagway in order to hike the Chilkoot Trail. For me, it was the highlight of our Alaskan trip, surpassing even the bears at Katmai. Beginning in 1896, the Klondike gold-rushers traveled the Chilkoot Trail to get to the gold fields in the Yukon. The Royal Canadian Mounted Police required every prospector to bring a list of supplies whose weight totaled more than one ton. There were several ways to accomplish this—a prospector could carry 50-pound payloads 40 times across the pass from Skagway to the Yukon; pay human "mules" to carry the cargo across at a cost of about one dollar a pound (approximately $2,000), or purchase expensive supplies from merchants at boomtowns along the way. The Klondike gold-rushers risked everything—their lives and their fortunes.

SUPPLIES FOR ONE MAN FOR ONE YEAR

Recommended by the Northern Pacific railroad company in the Chicago Record's Book for Gold Seekers, 1897

150 lbs. bacon	Two axes for four men and one extra handle
400 lbs. flour	Six 8 inch files and two taper files for the party
25 lbs. rolled oats	Draw knife, brace and bits, jack plane, and hammer for party 200 feet three-eights-inch rope
125 lbs. beans	8 lbs. of pitch and 5 lbs. of oakum for four men
10 lbs. tea	Nails, five lbs. each of 6,8,10 and 12 penny, for four men
10 lbs. coffee	Tent, 10 x 12 feet for four men
25 lbs. sugar	Canvas for wrapping
25 lbs. dried potatoes	Two oil blankets to each boat
2 lbs. dried onions	5 yards of mosquito netting for each man
15 lbs. salt, 1 lb. pepper	3 suits of heavy underwear
75 lbs. dried fruits	1 heavy mackinaw coat
8 lbs. baking powder	2 pairs heavy machinaw trousers
2 lbs. soda	1 heavy rubber-lined coat
1/2 lb. evaporated vinegar	1 dozen heavy wool socks
12 oz. compressed soup	1/2 dozen heavy wool mittens
1 can mustard	2 heavy overshirts
1 tin matches (for four men)	2 pairs heavy snagproof rubber boots
Stove for four men	2 pairs shoes
Gold pan for each	4 pairs blankets (for two men)
Set granite buckets	4 towels
Large bucket	2 pairs overalls
Knife, fork, spoon, cup, and plate	1 suit oil clothing
Frying pan	Several changes of summer clothing
Coffee and teapot	Small assortment of medicines
Scythe stone	
Two picks and one shovel	
One whipsaw	
Pack strap	

Source: National Park Service Website
http://www.nps.gov/klgo/learn/historyculture/tonofgoods.htm

We climbed through thick woodlands into sparse alpine highlands, then the barren uplands and ice fields to the base of the pass, up and across that rocky pass, down again until, at last, a long, gentle walk down toward the ghost town rail station at Bennett.

THE ELFIN
FOREST ALONG
THE CHILKOOT
TRAIL, ALASKA

I loved everything about the Chilkoot Trail. It took us five days. We started near sea level in the Alaskan rain forest, crossed marshes on walkways made from a line of slippery springy boards—rangers gleefully shared that other rangers had fallen off these boards into the marsh (although none admitted to falling themselves). Then we hiked up through mystical gardens of mosses and lichens that glowed brilliantly in the sunlight beneath the trees. I felt like I was a child peeking into a magical elfin world. We climbed through thick woodlands into sparse alpine highlands, then the barren uplands and ice fields to the base of the pass, up and across that rocky pass, down again until, at last, a long, gentle walk down toward the ghost town rail station at Bennett.

Two hikers fell through the ice that day going over the pass. The first was lucky. His leg met open air beneath the ice and he escaped unharmed. No one went to help him for fear of falling through the ice ourselves. The second wasn't lucky. A rock cut a long gash in the side of one leg. He stopped the bleeding, cleaned the wound, and then finished the hike. If a hiker was seriously injured, a helicopter ride out cost $2,500, more if the person needed to be flown to the hospital at Juneau.

The park service allows a maximum of 50 hikers to start the Chilkoot each day. We met five who turned back in the first two days. A woman injured her knee; consequently, she and her two companions turned back. A couple turned back when his down sleeping bag got soaked.

It rained for four of the five days that we hiked the Chilkoot Trail, the first two days almost constantly. Triveni was a trooper, she pushed on without a complaint. She seemed miserable. She walked deliberately with a serious look on her face, as if she were deep in thought. But I didn't let it bother me. I was having the best time of my life, which in retrospect probably only aggravated matters. Wrapped up in my own experience and by the physical challenge, I was being inconsiderate toward her and others. Perhaps I thought she was the experienced one, but I realize now she needed more encouragement and support from me. Yet, there is only so much one hiker can do for another. No one can walk the distance for you. In the end, you make the hike what you want it to be. Thankfully, the rain did stop the day we crossed the pass. I would not want to clamber up those rocks when they were wet.

THE VIEW LOOKING
BACK TOWARD
SKAGWAY: A BLUE
GLACIER ON THE
RIGHT; DARK,
CRAGGY MOUNTAINS
UP TO THE LEFT;
AND THE LONG
TRAIL BACK DOWN
THE NARROW, GREEN
VALLEY ALONG
A STREAM.

We crossed a series of ice fields before arriving at the foot of the pass. The pass itself is a notch between two mountain peaks, ascending almost one-third of a mile in almost one-third of a mile, over a pile of rocks and boulders. After a pair of false summits, there are additional ice fields. It was a hard climb, and to be honest, I crawled most of the way. I wore a video camera on my head to film my climb. The video portion is rather boring. All you can see is rock after rock in front of me, at my feet or slightly above me. At one point, a rock came lose in my hand, leaving the rocks above in abeyance. I quickly put it back in place before proceeding.

The audio portion of the video is more entertaining. I proceeded through something resembling stages of grief: a short period of denial, "This won't be hard, it doesn't look that far, lots of people do this"; rapidly followed by a lengthy period of obscenity-laden anger, mostly at myself for getting into this mess; then a period of bargaining with myself, "You can rest half-way, a third of the way..."; then a short period of largely silent depression; until finally grim acceptance, "You're not going back and the pass isn't going away. You might as well get on with it." It was a sequence of emotions I would become familiar with while becoming accustomed to hiking the Appalachian Trail.

About halfway up, I paused to rest and looked back toward Skagway. It was a magnificent view. A dog came to sit by me, also looking back. I appreciated the sentiment of sharing that glorious view across species, but when I turned to look at her, the poor dog was shivering, either from the cold, exhaustion, and/or fright, mirroring my own condition. When she reached the first ice field above, she ran and rolled around as happy as a puppy. Never had I seen a dog celebrate as enthusiastically. I almost joined her celebration, but there were two more summits to go. There were only two choices, move forward or go back and I was not about to turn around and head for Skagway in defeat. I would see it through.

Over the top, there were more ice fields and a long hike to the next camp site. At the end of that day, I was totally exhausted and went to bed without supper and missed the celebration in the hut that night.

The next two days were easier. When we arrived at Bennett to catch the train to Skagway, we odorous hikers had our own room around the back, far away from the other, less-fragrant patrons. I never had a more welcome meal: the best all-you-can-eat beef stew imaginable, baskets of bread, salad, coffee, and milk.

For a moment, we became celebrities when a few of the tourists started asking questions and taking pictures of us with our packs. I noted they kept their distance and stood upwind of us.

After lunch we hikers got onto our own train cars for the ride into Skagway, partially paralleling sections of the trail we had just hiked in the reverse direction. Although the scenery was beautiful, it rained most of the way back. Later we heard that Skagway had received more rain in those first two days than in the rest of the summer thus far.

Despite the Chilkoot, or rather because of the Chilkoot, I was hooked on hiking and camping. Triveni, however, looked away and said she was done with it. Now I think she meant more than hiking.

AFTER THE SUMMIT,
THE WAY OUT IN
CANADA

My grandmother used to say, "You never really know someone until you live with them," although I'm fairly certain she was referring to post-marriage acclimation and not recommending pre-marital cohabitation. Since returning from Alaska, I have heard others say that if you really want to know whether you can live together, take a long vacation together.

Triveni and I were adjusting to living together and doing so in an 8-by-23 foot box. For the most part, we worked well together, cooperating and dividing tasks fairly evenly. However, we were discovering differences between us that made our trip difficult. For example, she was a night person, while I was a morning person. For some reason, my noise making in the morning annoyed her more than hers at night bothered me. Initially, I did most of the driving and controlled the music and book selection when I drove, but agreed to relinquish control to her when she drove. We both liked the music from our youth and popular music, but I enjoyed listening to a wider range of music, such as alternative/punk, Euro-pop, and music from ethnic groups around the world, music that she didn't care for. I found the range of her selections to be limited, but didn't say anything. Perhaps being confined together all day long magnified these and other differences, but it was becoming apparent that we might never live together successfully without significant adjustments by each of us. These, however, were symptoms, there were more serious issues that we needed to discuss.

Reality
I promise to respect your family:
I'll be good to your mother,
listen to your father's stories
and be nice to your crazy sister.

I'll to be the one you drag to the ballet,
reminding me I promised, "someday."
I'll hold your bags and be your valet,
and listen to how I should spend Saturday.

I promise to stand close to the toilet,
and try to hit the target.
I'll clean up the mess, when I miss,
and, oh yes, remember to put down the seat.

I'll leave my chair when you call, "Come, look at that"
and lie when you ask, "Does this make me look fat?"
I'll let you lift snacks from my bowl
and even let you have the remote control.

There is one thing I have to ask.
I want to hear all you have to say,
but right now, I just want to relax,
so, honey, could we please save it for another day?

⁂

With hindsight, I'm able to see that in contrast to the experience of trekking, when becoming comfortable would lead me to experience new and richer dimensions of the Trail, it seemed that Triveni and I were growing apart during our immersion. Oh, we had a good time, laughing and joking, and did all of the things that close friends on a tour might do. We traveled, ate, hung out, and went on excursions together. We shared the experience, but we were not sharing ourselves. Something was missing between us.

Look into My Eyes

Why don't you kiss me, like you did before?
Why don't you tell me that you love me anymore?

Look into my eyes like you did once before,
when you held my hands and to love me swore
through life, forever after and more.

When you led me onto the dance floor
spinning me to display the glory I wore,
lifting me above the wooden floor,
holding me there while my heart and soul did soar
in joy, leaving me to hover o'er.

Slowly you lowered me to the floor,
whispered an overture,
and whisked me out the hotel door.

Look into my eyes once more,
show me the man I did adore,
and lead me to our bedroom door.

I should have seen the coming trouble.

ABOVE THE CLOUDS, NORTH OF LAMBERTS MEADOW SHELTER, VIRGINIA

CHAPTER 7: *Sustenance*

If, of these, none,
neither love idyllic
nor moment vanishing,
not a habit, trick,
game or understanding,
what is left then but sentiment?

FUEL

In 2013, I was making good progress and keeping up with my friends on the Trail, but I was losing weight precipitously. All male through-hikers lose weight, whereas women, in accordance with another Trail saying, lose inches and gain muscle. In 2013, I lost over 40 pounds in 67 days. This was too much. I wasn't the only one losing weight. Olive Oyl suggested Slim change his name to "Emaciated." Danno said he lost 70 pounds by Katahdin.

I simply couldn't eat enough. I hadn't found a menu that gave me the calories necessary to do the miles I was covering. My daughters were mailing me healthy dehydrated meals that I couldn't stomach so I traded or gave them away, except for the dehydrated pickles, which were incredible thin strips of concentrated pickle-ness. These healthy foods filled my stomach but my hunger remained. Instead I craved foods I ordinarily never ate, such as summer sausages and potted meats. Splurging in town helped, but I could never make up what I was losing on the Trail.

Ultimately, I ran out of my reserves. I walked into camp shivering until I ate something. My body needed fuel immediately. That's what did me in, not eating enough to hike the miles I was doing. Eventually I got sick, and that was the end of 2013. I had sabotaged myself, pushing too hard and doing too many miles for the calories I was consuming.

Why was I pushing myself so hard? In part, I tried to keep up with the crowd of people I knew. Also, I felt pressure from being behind my planned schedule and not wanting to fall further behind. But more importantly, I fell prey to perhaps the greatest threat to a trekker: boredom. Quickly tiring of the routine in town: shower, eat, stop in at a bar to see who was in town,

He was overloaded, clanked with each step, and even carried a solar panel on his back to charge the battery to his laptop while he hiked.

sleep, eat, do laundry, eat, resupply, eat, phone home, write letters and transcribe the latest versions of my poems, eat, watch some TV, eat and back to the bar, and so forth, I'd move on. I wasn't eating or resting enough.

My system simply couldn't process the amount of food I needed to consume each day. At 40 pounds lost, if not more, in 67 days, I was expending 2,000 calories more than I was consuming each day. I needed almost 6,000 calories a day, whereas I was eating less than 4,000.

Six thousand calories is a lot of food. Peanut butter is one of the densest calorie foods at 150 calories per ounce, thus 6,000 calories of peanut butter weighs 2.5 pounds, but man cannot live on peanut butter alone. Six thousand calories of high-calorie food typically weighs more than three pounds. That's a lot to carry and to eat, day after day.

Standing in a market, I compared packets of foods. How many calories per ounce, how much protein, did it even appeal to me? French fried onions were great to add to a meal. Because I tired of whatever I ate, I varied the selection and ratios of nuts, candies, dried fruits, protein bars, meats, crackers, and cookies. Dried dates and figs were awesome. My mouth still moistens at the thought of dates.

The conundrum for trekkers is that while the body needs to maintain its weight, carrying excess weight in supplies and equipment can defeat the best of hikers. It is hard to overstate the challenge of carried weight, even for the young. I learned a military saying, "Ounces equal pounds and pounds equal pain." One young man who was just starting out, hiking south from Waynesboro, Virginia, reconsidered his excursion as he balked at his first cliff walk. He was overloaded, clanked with each step, and even carried a solar panel on his back to charge the battery to his laptop while he hiked. Yes, he carried a laptop, the charger, and a backup external drive for his files. I can't imagine what else he had inside his large backpack, but he had a pot and a cup hanging on the outside. We started toward Waynesboro together, but he couldn't keep up with me. Finally I had met someone slower than me! He was a fit young man in his early twenties, defeated by his overflowing backpack.

At three-plus pounds a day, a five-day supply of food weighs 16 pounds. Toss in three liters of water and 18 pounds of gear means carrying 40 pounds leaving town and an average weight of 29 pounds (half of water and food consumed at midpoint). I knew I couldn't carry that much weight and do the miles needed to reach Katahdin. By timing myself, I discovered that a 30-pound load increased the time required to reach a prescribed distance from an hour to an hour and a half. Hiking longer hours would increase the need for calories. Either I needed to hike fewer miles in a day or find a better diet.

In 2014, I changed my approach to food. I knew I couldn't eat enough, my stomach wouldn't cooperate. Instead, I resolved to drink more calories and increase my snacking. I started carrying dehydrated whole milk and powdered sports drinks. In the morning, a pint of whole milk got me off to a good start, and another pint or two sustained my energy through the day and night. I drank the sports drink instead of water. These two measures added more than 1,000 calories a day to my diet.

In addition to the snacks I ordinarily consumed, I filled reusable squeeze tubes with peanut butter. I carried one of these tubes in a pocket and every once in a while, squeezed a line of peanut butter into my mouth. This added several hundred more calories in a day, but I haven't eaten peanut butter since.

I began to take advantage of every restaurant and shop near the Trail. In the South, towns and shops were farther apart, but as I moved north, there were more opportunities to jump on and off the Trail quickly, meaning I could carry less food. The 2,000 calories in a large Italian deli sub loaded with dressing and mayonnaise plus the accompanying chips, soda, and brownie were well worth walking a mile or more to a country store or town. If hiking to and from a deli burned 600 calories, the meal itself put me in the black by 1,400 calories, which was the equivalent of three-quarters of a pound of trail food. If I resupplied at the deli, I could start out carrying less weight.

Even with the milk, sports drink, peanut butter, and delis, for five days of hiking I needed to carry 10 or more pounds of food. The only solution to lowering my pack weight was to eliminate every fraction of an ounce from my pack and carry less water.

I had done a fairly good job at limiting my gear before starting in 2013, but for 2014, I looked closely at everything, including what I was wearing, my poles, and what I had in my pockets. In 2014, I reduced my total carry by two pounds five ounces of winter gear and almost five pounds of summer gear, despite using a larger net tent, a heavier duty garbage bag for my pack cover, switching to the heavier biodegradable wipes for cleaning, and adding a GPS tracker.

For 2015, before food and water but including fuel, my winter (March) total carry weighed 24 pounds 9 ounces and summer (May) total carry at 19 pounds 13 ounces, with a summer pack weight of 15 pounds. I have eliminated almost five pounds in winter weight and seven pounds in summer weight.

Between the drinks, peanut butter tubes, and other diet changes in 2014, I cut my weight loss from more than 40 pounds in 2013 to a more tolerable 15 pounds. In 2013, I had lost more than a half pound per day; in 2014 I lost only a quarter pound a day. Even at that rate, I would lose 50 pounds over a through-hike, which might be tolerable, if I rested longer and ate more in town to compensate.

Alas, if only that weight stayed off. When you leave the Trail, your appetite stays with you. In 2013, I put on a pound a day my first two weeks home.

MY CURRENT GEAR

My goal is a starting total carry of 33 pounds, for an average of 25.5 pounds over a five-day hiking session. If I stopped for water more often and if I drank at least a pint of water when filling up, I might carry no more than 2.5 liters, weighing five pounds. If I carried 13 pounds of food, that left me with 15 pounds for everything else: clothes; water filter; stove, fuel, pot, and utensils; tarp, net tent, stakes and lines; food bag and line to hang; ground cover, sleeping bag and pad; first aid and hygiene; maps and guides; sunscreen and bug spray; phone, camera, and charger, the GPS locator, odds and ends and the backpack itself.

Backpack	Summer Weight	Extra Winter Weight
Total ounces	243.1	48.0
pounds	15.0	3.0
ounces	3.0	0.0
Carry: backpack, rain-cover, hip pocket	38.7	
Shelter: tarp, net tent, stakes, lines, ground cover	45.4	
Sleep: sleeping bag, liner, emergency blanket, bivy, sleep pad	36.7	31.0
Hydration: filter, chemicals, water bag, bottles	7.8	
Kitchen: stove, cup, fuel, utensil, blade	6.4	
Food Storage: food bag and hang line	4.1	
Extra Sleep Clothes: shirt, long underwear, cap	18.0	0.3
Change of Clothes: compression shorts, sock, liners, shirt, shorts	12.0	3.7

Outerwear: gloves, glove liners, earmuffs, rain pants, rain jacket	8.4	12.7
Hygiene: trowel, toilet paper, flosser, toothbrush, toothpaste, towel, soap, comb	18.6	
Meds: first aid and pills	3	
Repair kit	0.6	
Preventative: bug lotion, spray, lubricant, sunscreen	8.7	
Extra glasses	1.7	
Electronics: camera, lights, charger and cords, cell phone, phone cover	20.0	
Navigation: pen, maps, GPS, compass	10.2	
Paper and pen	2.5	
Clothes I wear or carry, not included above:	54.3	40.8
Trekking poles	18.7	
Emergency: whistle, mirror, fire starter	1.2	
Grand Total Weight	305.1	88.5
Pounds	19.0	6.0

When people ask me about my experience hiking the Trail, I am more than happy to tell them. Many people don't have any idea of what it is like. They ask, "Where do you stay?" Some seem astounded at the thought of sleeping in a tent most of the time, carrying your food, and filtering water. Little kids often ask, "Where do you go to the bathroom?" The thought of walking as many as 20 miles on some days is as incomprehensible to most people as it was to me at one time, but they know instinctively that it is not easy.

After listening for a while, they often ask, "Why do you do this to yourself?"

The joy and sheer pleasure of it is worth everything I've endured. Although it's often challenging, the rewards, such as the sights seen, wildlife encountered, and friendships forged, can be great. Also, the opportunity to reflect and to write is unmatched.

Why Hike?

It has to do with moonlight,
and stars on a moonless night,
with a tree in silhouette
against a moonlit cloud;

It has to do with sunlight
revealing the morning's heights
and sunbeams parting a mist
to light a bush in flowers shrouded;

With stopping on a grassy bald
to see mountains as islands
rising above the great green deep
and a town small with the world wide around;

With clouds quickly rippling treble
to ridges playing a rumbling bass
in a chord struck by a mighty hammer
hitting distant ground;

With resting atop a mountain
to see the clouds and rain
from which we have just escaped,
then rise once more to go down;

To be surprised by a bear
approaching my lonely shelter,
checking for leftovers
before turning and bounding away;

To hear a grouse thumping
like a helicopter accelerating
and at night coyotes everywhere around
then a dying sound;

To find a deer and fawn
cautious statues silently appraising
from a field of ferns emerging
fiddleheads still tightly bound;

To see dew drops' translucent sheen
on a web cast in silver
and creatures more perfect than figurines,
an artist's hands confounded;

To walk along a ridgeline,
not a flower to be seen
but their fragrance carried by updrafts,
walking in a perfumed cloud;

To meet with people you like
and in the morning hike
until the trail separates
then at day's end, friends gladly found.

Some days can be described as "supernatural." April 21, 2104, was perfect for hiking: cool, dry, and sunny. The views were wonderful and the trail a good hike. At Bird's Nest Shelter, Virginia, a south-bound couple was hiking to lose weight for their upcoming wedding. After descending from Mary's Rock, while I was waiting at the parking lot, milepost 937, for a shuttle driver to take me into Luray, Virginia, a leather-clad motorcyclist couple asked me to take their picture. They had just gotten engaged.

CLOUDS RIPPLING
TREBLE, JAMES RIVER
AREA, VIRGINIA

UNDERNOURISHED

After completing the Chilkoot Trail, Triveni and I drove north from Skagway before turning south on the Cassiar Highway, which runs parallel to the Pacific Coast, to Hider, Alaska. From there we motored east to Jasper, the Icefield Parkway, and Banff. Outside the truck was beautiful country and wonderful weather; inside the cab, long periods of cold quiet. Neither of us wanted to start our long-overdue conversation, fearful of how it might end.

Stark is the Silence

Stark is the silence
when we are alone,
lost is the innocence
we had known.

Where once attention
had affection shown,
now their absence
weighs like a stone.

What explains the distance
that has grown,
the consequence
of what we had sown

and negligence
at what we allowed to grow?
Only prudence
against angry words

over some grievance
for which we must atone;
all the arguments
we chose to postpone,

their importance
thought overblown
until avoidance
became the cornerstone

to maintaining the balance
of our home.
Once but an annoyance
we did condone,

now their omittance
has replaced what we had owned
with indifference
worse than callous words.

Stark is the silence
when we are alone.
Lost is the romance
we had known.

❧

At Banff, I went for a hike while Triveni stayed behind to rest, watch TV and call her friends. I walked for a while with two lady hikers. I told them I was with my fiancée but I thought it was over between us. She had changed the background picture on her laptop: the picture of our engagement had been replaced by a picture of a bear.

FOLLOW THE BLAZE: BEFORE THE AUDIE MURPHY MONUMENT, VIRGINIA

CHAPTER 8: *Losses*

A lasting gift
that cannot be purchased,
only given,
sometimes squandered,
often neglected and forgotten,
but patiently persistent.

LEAVING THE TRAIL

I hate hiking in heavy rain, much worse than in snow or heat. Growing up and living in snow country for most of my life, I'm used to dealing with the snow and cold, and quickly adapted to the snow along the Appalachian Trail in March of 2013 and 2014. As long as I was careful not to risk hypothermia by overheating, which would cause me to sweat and then chill my core, and as long as I stayed warm at night, the cold wasn't dangerous.

Not that I enjoyed hiking in high temperatures under a strong sun along an exposed ridgeline blown by winds that sucked every bit of moisture out of me. If I stayed hydrated, maintained my electrolytes, covered my head, and lathered myself in sunscreen, I might be exhausted by the end of the day, but I was OK.

There was a Trail saying, "No rain, no pain, no Maine," but I really hated hiking in the rain. It is not the light or even moderate rain, which cools the air and makes hiking more comfortable, that I hate. It's not the slipping, sliding, and falling, so that by the end of the day everything is coated by mud, that I hate. No, what I hate is the way rain chills me deep inside more than any snowstorm, no matter how frigid the temperature might be. Almost any rain can kill you, draining the heat from you and leading to hypothermia.

In heavy rain, no matter how careful, I got wet, if not from the rain, from overheating encased in my protective rain gear. Once wet, I began to chill. I had a small taste of hypothermia once when I reached the top of the Chilkoot Pass in Alaska. My clothes were sweaty and the wind was strong. The cold reached inside like an icy hand toward my heart. It was colder and, I sensed, more deadly than any other cold I had experienced. I quickly took off my wet clothes, cooked a hot meal of oatmeal and a warm drink, and accepted a warming chemical packet from some Canadians.

You might skip hiking on rainy days, but you can't stay in town all the time, so eventually you will get caught in a heavy rain. By watching others, I subsequently learned to avoid overheating by ditching my rain pants, and accepting muddy legs and possibly wet feet. To keep from chilling my core, I wore a wool shirt beneath my rain jacket, because wool retains most of its ability to preserve heat even when it is wet. And after that experience at Chilkoot, I immediately get out of my wet clothes when I stop moving.

MODESTY

On Trail, almost everyone was modest. Usually hikers would change in their tents or a privy, go behind a shelter or a bush, or retreat to a dark corner in a shelter. Sometimes, someone would announce that they were about to change so that others could turn away. Once a hiker invited to laughter, "I'm changing; don't look if you don't want to," before adding, "I didn't mean that the way it sounded." Eventually I became adept at changing inside my sleeping bag. But not everyone was so modest.

Oh, to be a Ferret
Oh, to be a ferret
with a furry coat
and wear it
as an overcoat,
no need for a closet
just wear it as a housecoat,
quite adequate
even as a raincoat,
wear it everywhere on autopilot
but I don't need to gloat.

After a couple days of rain, every piece of clothing was too wet to dry inside my sleeping bag. I tried my best to dry out my clothes at night, but often they were still damp in the morning. I really hated putting on wet hiking clothes in the morning. The wool quickly warmed up but was uncomfortable, and the dampness irritated my skin. Everything began to stink. One night I said to Olive Oyl, Wet Bag, and Otto, "I smell like a swamp." They laughed and said they did too.

My boots and feet stayed dry because I used a large, heavy garbage bag as a rain cover for my backpack. The rain ran down and out onto the scallop-shaped tops of the garbage bag and flipped away from my legs and feet while I walked. A heavy-duty garbage bag weighed a bit less than a regular rain cover, and it stayed put through heavy winds because I cut slots in the bag for the shoulder straps. Rain covers had been lifted off packs and blown away by strong winds. The plastic garbage bag pressed against my back by the pack made me too hot, which I solved by cutting a window in the bag for my back.

I also used the cyclists' lubricant on my feet the night before rain. It works best applied at night to feet, thighs, and other areas so that it penetrates the skin and dries by morning. Otherwise, the lotion saturates socks or shorts and leaves the socks and shorts stiff when it dries.

On May 17, 2013, I joined Olive Oyl, Wet Bag, and Otto. It was good to be with people I knew and liked. In the morning, I left early hoping to cross a rocky slanted cliff walk before the rain started.

It started to pour as I neared the Audie Murphy Monument at Brush Mountain in Virginia. I was soaked by the time we camped by Trout Creek. Scout troops had filled the shelter and campsites ahead. In the morning, my clothes were still wet. The next day, I was soaked under my rain jacket by Dragon's Tooth on Cove Mountain and it was raining again. To go down from Dragon's Tooth, I needed to turn to the left between two rocks. The white blaze marking the Appalachian Trail was between those rocks.

LAST VIEW IN 2013, FROM HAY ROCK, BEFORE DESCENDING INTO DALEVILLE, VIRGINIA

I missed it. Up Hill said he had missed it years before. Instead, I went straight ahead, climbing down a series of difficult descents over wet rocks in the rain. Not impossibly difficult for the Appalachian Trail, after all, I thought, this section was supposed to be challenging, until I reached an impasse. There was no clear direction down over even more difficult and dangerous-looking damp descents.

I struggled back up the hard climb until I saw a white blaze pointing in the direction from which I had come. I didn't see an option from the direction in which I was going, so I climbed back down, looked it over again, and rejected it. Then I worked my way back up, then down and back up one more time before sitting to wait for someone to come along.

Eventually, a group showed up and explained I had taken a wrong turn. "Lots of people do that here," they said, pointing me in the right direction. The way down from Dragon's Tooth was wet, but at least the rain had reduced to a drizzle. I don't remember much about the descent, except that at several points I had to lower my backpack before I could climb down myself. After the wrong path I had taken, it seemed easy to me. When I reached the road, I was shivering. I started toward a nearby convenience store where I could warm up and get a couple of cheeseburgers, when a hosteller picked me up in his truck, took me to first his hostel and then to an all-you-can-eat restaurant for dinner.

> For some reason, I found it easier to work on a poem while I was walking than sitting in a room staring at a wall or a computer screen.

By the time I got to Daleville, Virginia, I was feverish and once started, I couldn't stop coughing. Walking to a restaurant across the street from the motel exhausted me. It was time to leave the Trail. My friends encouraged me to rest a while, to see if I recovered and changed my mind. I rested for three days, wavering between continuing and leaving. Then I received a call and headed home.

Otis

When I got to Daleville,
I couldn't go any further.
So I took a few days to rest,
then got a call from mother.
I rented a car
to go help move her.
What else can one do,
but lend a hand to your brothers?

OTIS

When I got there, I was sick
and needed time to recover,
so wasn't much help
moving mother.
I got my truck to take some items
back for my daughters,
then twisted my knee,
and was through helping my brothers.

I headed home again,
this time to see my doctor.
I was stuck there in therapy,
but had Father's Day with my daughters
and with Otis, our basset hound,
who seemed much older
and, hard to believe, even slower.

But with us all together,
he did seem happier.

Otis and I took long walks together,
rested in the shade side by side,
and napped next to each other,
me on the couch
and him on the floor,
until one morning he collapsed
and died in five hours.

When I had left months before
I had told him not to die
while I was away.
So now I wonder
had he been waiting,
obedient one last time
and if so, did he suffer?

Although I miss him greatly,
we had a few weeks together.
I suppose one can't hope for more
when time is shorter than longer.
It seems like a chain now:
one thing leading to another—
illness, mother, and knee—
to an ending for Otis and me.

I left the Trail because I was sick, because my mother was moving, and for one more reason: to begin this book. Back in Hot Springs, I had found inspiration for writing. The longer I hiked, the more important writing became and the less important the Trail. Still, I resisted leaving the Trail until I felt an obligation to help my mother. Once I left the Trail, writing became my occupation, filling my nights and days until I returned to the Trail in 2014.

Now, I wonder whether writing made me inattentive to trekking, my health, and nutrition. If I hadn't spent so much time dreaming about a book, might I have remained healthy and gone further?

For some reason, I found it easier to work on a poem while I was walking than sitting in a room staring at a wall or a computer screen. Looking back, I had hiked for nine days straight without rest at the end of my 2013 hike, which was foolish. I had simply lost track of what I was doing. I had become a walking automaton.

At times on the Trail, I would speak fragments of a poem to myself, as if I were talking to an imaginary friend, because as someone once said, the ear is the best judge of words.

Sometimes, when I focused on a poem, I'd wander off-trail. I would have to retrace my steps to find the Appalachian Trail again. I climbed Wesser Bald in North Carolina twice this way, first on one trail and then again on the Appalachian Trail. These off-trail excursions shortened as I developed a sense of when I was on the Trail and when not. Suddenly, I would stop to look around for a reassuring white blaze. When necessary, I dropped my pack to run ahead or back to find a white blaze. Even in 2014, my mind wandered off-trail, taking me with it. There was one 16-mile section in Pennsylvania where I missed two parts, completely. I hiked the distance, just not on the Appalachian Trail for those miles. I'll have to go back and re-hike that section of the Trail someday.

I must have seemed to be an odd fellow to some hikers, distracted and in my own world. My daughters say that I live in a different world, looking at things in a different way. I realize now it is inspiration.

At times on the Trail, I would speak fragments of a poem to myself, as if I were talking to an imaginary friend, because as someone once said, the ear is the best judge of words. Somehow the physical exertion of the Trail made it easier for the words expressing emotions and thoughts to surface. They kept distracting me, not only while hiking, but in shelters, hostels, restaurants, and bars, even during a pause in conversation. My mind was elsewhere—not a good thing while hiking.

BREAKING UP

Triveni and I had been innocently enjoying the company of others, but we were also avoiding each other. We needed space between us. Spending time away from each other is necessary to a healthy relationship; it allows each person to recharge their batteries. However, neither Triveni nor I were making an effort to arrange special moments together anymore. While we were apart, alternatives presented themselves, opportunities arose, and the possibility of change occurred to me and, I believe, to her as well. Were we becoming distracted?

The situation was like when we were on the Chilkoot Trail. We were in different places. I was trying to make the most of the experience, while she seemed eager for it to be over.

At dinner one night in Alaska, a woman squeezed my upper arm. When I turned toward her, she winked. I did not respond, but Triveni witnessed the entire episode. We never spoke about it.

Now, I'm not used to women making passes at me. I'm not that good looking; I'm clearly aging, I'm not fashionable, nor am I rich or famous. In Alaska, the odds actually appeared to be in a woman's favor. There were many more men than women about. Perhaps I was a ticket out of Alaska? Had I been sending signals of availability? Ominously, I thought of possible endings to our relationship.

Differently
(Things might have been different,
if only I had two lives to live:
one for you and one for him.)

> *(If I had taken more care,*
> *then things might have ended differently,*
> *but some things cannot be shared,*

> *words unsaid or deeds undone.)*
I want you to know I love you both;
It wasn't just for the fun.

> *Which do you think might hurt less:*
> *to lose your love casually*
> *or more thoughtfully?*

Or neglected thoughtlessly?
> *Sorry. Once upon a time we did love...*
We did, but now we must move on.

Tell me, do you believe in destiny,
something about you and me,
something to our chemistry?

> *Do you mean, if we could turn back time*
> *and live our lives more carefully,*
> *might things turn out differently?*

When I went for coffee one night, Triveni again stayed in our room in town to rest and work on her computer. I discovered musicians playing nearby. I lingered and began talking with several young women, one of whom stayed with me when the others left. Nothing untoward happened between us, only pleasant conversation about our trips to Alaska and lives in the lower 48. But I stayed longer than I should have.

At the Office

My dear, how much can I trust
you to have been at the office,
when it's much too late for that
and I can smell cigarettes and alcohol?

My dear, how many times must
we have this conversation?
When you're going to be late,
you know I'll worry, why don't you just call?

My dear, while you're staying out late,
having fun at breakfast,
I'm home all alone.
I'm through talking to our bedroom wall.

What is tonight's excuse, my dearest?
I must have heard them all by now.
We are so well practiced,
do you need say anything at all?

You wear your innocence well,
but I know much more than you think
and now your fear does betray you.
Exactly how far, my dear, did you fall?

⁂

When we reached Calgary on our way back to Michigan, Triveni and I broke up on the first anniversary of our engagement, short-circuiting my plans of commemoration for the evening. I finally criticized her limited taste in music—and we were off. Things were said: some true, others exaggerated, malicious, and untrue. Some words cannot be taken back or forgiven easily. That would require time to heal. While we needed to have a serious sit-down, the timing made me angry. And in my anger, I decided against trying to save our relationship by being the first to apologize, which only worsened

ICEFIELDS HIGHWAY,
BRITISH COLUMBIA
AND ALBERTA

the situation. We reached an impasse; it was over. Instead of stopping in Calgary, I drove straight through. There was no reason to stop anymore.

How had our relationship collapsed? I don't intend to assume or assign blame. If, in some ways or at some times, I was more at fault than she, the same was true for her. Triveni and I were partners in the demise of our relationship.

Initially, we both got caught up in a dream, wanting to believe that we had found someone to love for the rest of our lives. It didn't become clear to me until later, that we had started to pull back from each other almost immediately after our engagement in 2010 but especially during the early months of 2011.

In retrospect, it seems that we decided to stop working on our relationship. Although we had talked about long-term goals, we still had a lot of issues to work out before we could marry. We both began to have doubts. That is normal, I think, to take a step forward and then to reconsider. It is part of the process of working things out: you discover issues and talk about them. But we never did talk.

All of these details and questions might have been resolved, but buying the trailer had been a crucial mistake. With the trailer, we were financially obligated to each other and committed to our trip to Alaska. What would we do with the trailer we had just purchased if we broke up? I had raised the stakes by proposing, and Triveni had doubled down with the trailer, before we were really ready to make such serious commitments.

In anticipation of our excursion, we bit our tongues. We let things slide rather than deal with them. Without the trailer, we might have worked things out or broken up earlier. While a trailer wasn't as large an obligation as buying a house or having a child together, we had boxed ourselves in. It wasn't a conscious decision to not talk about issues, more like a decision not to rock the boat.

During our trip, more issues came up that we needed to discuss, but we did not. Neither one of us wanted to disrupt the trip, detracting from our enjoyment and perhaps jeopardizing its completion. Time and again, when we needed to have a serious discussion, we chose to avoid it. I have visual memories of Triveni and of the two of us doing things together on our trip to Alaska, but I cannot remember a single serious conversation between us during the trip, until the breakup.

The drive from Michigan through Alaska and ending in Calgary haunted me for a long time. What had begun so wonderfully, ended so poorly.

The Road to Calgary (completed)
I drive rising, rolling hills
dotted by bushes and trees
toward evergreen forests and mountains.
I dream I drive the road to Calgary.

Looking back, I can see now that our precious trip had become more important to us than our relationship. We were focused on our next Great Adventure, the trip to Alaska, which we had both wanted to complete, when we should have focused more on our Greater Adventure, our relationship, if there was going to be something more than one adventure. It was like parents who focus on their children while neglecting their partner or like fathers and mothers who focus on providing for the family while neglecting other requirements. Like any of us needing more balance in our lives.

I cannot help but contrast this breakup to my divorce. Because we had children together, my ex-wife and I had an incentive to come to a workable arrangement. If imperfectly, we continued to talk throughout our marriage, during the divorce, and afterward. In the end, she and I realized we couldn't live together. We got divorced, but at least we talked through the process. We're not best buddies but we get along pretty well compared to some other divorced couples I know, and there remains affection between us. I'm thankful for that.

As I mentioned, Triveni and I had serious differences we needed to discuss. We had decided to go to Alaska as planned and postpone dealing with these matters until later. Perhaps we felt obligated to stay together through Alaska or maybe we both just wanted to go to Alaska at that point.

Our engagement was broken and our trip was over although there were hundreds of miles to go. We both had a lot of emotions to work through. It would be a long ride home.

Going Home
I've separated what's mine from yours,
looked in the bathroom and under the bed.
checked the closets and dresser drawers,

My bags are packed and waiting by the door.
I'll start putting things in the car
and go get us some drinks from the store.

Feels like I've been here before.
Like a favorite book that's been over-read,
the words don't seem to matter anymore.

The words are all so familiar.
I'm living in a cliché,
I've already heard everything we've had to say;

and the plot is so similar:
arrive in high gear, drive home in reverse.
Instead of a blessing, love has been a curse.

A new thought comes to me as we drive away:
when love is just like a vacation,
breaking up feels like going home.....

VIEW FROM THREE RIDGES, VIRGINIA

CHAPTER 9: *Fulfillment*

What if all,
not one or none, but each and every,
and more unspoken
or imagined,
ten thousand moments to love or end,
might that be love?

END OF THE TRAIL

In August 2013, Danno was nearing Katahdin, the end of the Appalachian Trail, but Slim had fallen behind. Slim kept leaving the Trail to attend family events. I joked to Slim that he might have the record for the most section hikes in one year. I heard from Slim that he was close behind Danno. I was excited for them and expressed a wish that they would summit together. Slim texted back, "I will see if I can make it happen." Slim hurried ahead while Danno waited for him. I didn't hear anything more for a few weeks until I received a picture of them leaning on the sign at the top of Katahdin. They had summited together.

Pictures quickly followed from Cruise and Corn Dog, Lady and Photo Bomber (Photo Bomber joined Lady in New England before turning south to finish in Virginia in late December), followed by Olive Oyl and Wet Bag, Waffles, and HoBo. Of the 13 trekkers with whom I remained in contact, 10 had made it to Katahdin. I tried to imagine what it must have been like.

On Katahdin
Before dawn, we rise
to climb our last mountain.
We scramble over rocks,
the peak our beacon.
We pause to say,
"We've been where you want to be,"
and shout, "Here we are!"

Scarcely a sound in the world,
but for us, silence all around,
we arrive at the crest.
Finding the highest ground,
we stand to say:
"We've done things you want to do,"
and shout, "Here we are!"

We cross a narrow ridgeline,
on either side a fantasia
of sky, water, hills, and valleys,
a portrait in God's chosen media.
We stop to say:
"We've seen sights you long to see,"
and shout, "Here we are!"

Some bright, early morning,
leave your campsite,
rise up to come hike with us,
so on that distant height
you can stand to say:
"I've been where you want to be,
I've done things you want to do,
and seen sights you long to see,"
then shout, "Here I am!"

From the pictures they sent, the women appeared to have fared better than the men. They looked trim, fit, and healthy, whereas the men all looked haggard. I had heard of this phenomenon. I think it has to do with women being smaller than men, thereby needing fewer calories and being able to satisfy more of their daily requirement by what they can carry. Even so, these were the tough women who had mastered the Trail.

Ladies of the Trail
It's easy to forget she's a lady:
When, for a couple of days, it's been raining,
feet are getting soft with blisters forming.
No one wants to get up in the morning
but she stands there waiting
for you to get your pack together.
She curses like a pro and not some amateur,
drinks her first beer like she's thirstier
than you are, then slows down for the long night haul.

Picks herself up from a fall,
cracking a joke that has us all
laughing. She carries on so ably,
you forget she's a lady,
but when she sets her place with a napkin,
tilts her head, and smiles so innocently,
you realize, she really is a lady.

COMPREHENSION

During the drive home from Calgary and afterwards, I tried to extract some meaning from my romantic love affair and engagement with Triveni. While my daughters were growing and even now, when they have a setback, I would emphasize to them, "It's only a mistake if you don't learn from it. Otherwise, it is a lesson."

So, what lessons have I learned about love and romance? Upon reflection, I realized that I had taken a long time to recover since my divorce. My path resembled the hierarchy of needs popularized by Maslow. I joke, only to myself, that the trail crossed Healing Knob, Mount Personal Growth, Peak Lust, and the dreaded range, Fear of Commitment. I began my quest with the most basic elements of male-female relationships, companionship and physical intimacy. Over time, I wanted more from a relationship. As a result, I became more selective in whom I would see and the relationships lasted longer. Now I am no longer content with good enough for now.

As for Triveni, it wasn't enough for us both to want a long-term relationship. It wasn't enough to make a promise to each other. We had to follow through, and that took effort. We didn't have the desire needed to put forth the effort to make the relationship work. In the end, our relationship became all about our adventures.

By the time things came to a head, there was too much for us to deal with all at once. Where did we begin? For every "this," there was a "that." All the slights, offenses, and issues presented at once were overwhelming, at least to me. Things were said and bridges were burned. There was no going back. Once we were apart, I don't think either of us gave any thought to trying to get back together; but then, we never talked about it.

What sustains a relationship is constant communication and negotiation. It is the oil the keeps the engine running. Not flowers and candy, not candlelit dinners, nor the scheduled and impromptu niceties, although they are necessary, and not all the other things that make a relationship. Ultimately, communication, the honest expression of disagreements, then resolution and reconciliation, all supported and maintained by a thing we call "love," that is what sustains a relationship and helps it to grow. In the process, while love grows deeper, each of us grows as a person.

I will continue to take the risk in the hope of finding one last true Great Adventure.

❧

The differences between us might have been truly insurmountable. By our neglect, however, we had squandered whatever chance we might have had to forge a lasting partnership. So if you ask me why it ended, there were a thousand reasons, but the only one that really mattered was we didn't talk about it until it was too late.

So, I had learned that love is not a place where a couple is joined; nor in words and promises no matter how holy; nor in a precious purpose, not even one accomplished according to plan, but in two joined heart and mind, body, and soul, despite obstacles, flaws, and imperfections, steadfast.

I already knew that; we all know that. It was in the fairy tales we were told as children and that we read to our children. It was in the movies we watched with them. Well, the beginning phase of love was portrayed in the books and movies, but not the rest, the part about living together. Falling in love is easy, living together day after day is hard, dealing with ten thousand reasons and opportunities to call it quits, and perhaps that is true love.

Where Does Love Reside?
Where does love reside,
in a book somewhere underlined,
inside a temple enshrined
or by a bedside?

Not in the here and now
in a well-spoken vow,
and not there and then
after the final amen;

Not in a plan well made,
in a schedule obeyed
against time constrained,
or at a destination attained;

Not in a place that cannot be seen
too small to find,
not hidden behind,
beyond or in between;

But within a woman and a man,
two hearts and minds conjoined,
two bodies intertwined
and two souls glorified.

⁂

It is rare to find true love. I have heard divorce lawyers doubt its existence at any age. I have met many women and men my age and, sadly, younger, both single and divorced, who have given up and just want to ease their way out of life like the old bears retreating to a comfortable place. As a barber, speaking for himself, asked, "How many times can you stand to have your heart be broken?"

Yet, I can't give up. I know I'm running out of time and I'm beginning to wonder whether it is even possible for me to live with anyone else, or more so her with me. I do enjoy the company of a woman, but I like my space and am content being able to purse my interests without interference, interruption, and compromise.

Ultimately, I may be disappointed. My heart may be broken when I fall short at my third attempt at romantic love. If so, I'll try a fourth. I will continue to take the risk in the hope of finding one last true Great Adventure.

STARTING IN 2014, A VIEW NORTH OF DALEVILLE, VIRGINIA

*A mystery,
a secret hidden from all
but its participants,
yet recognized
as present or absent
by the observant.*

A NEW START

I dropped Triveni off at an airport so she could fly home. It was what she wanted, but it precluded any further conversation once we had cooled down. We shared a moment of compassion for each other as we said good-bye. I kept the trailer because I planned to move it around Canada and the United States, staying in an area for two or three months in order to explore each place more completely. Triveni had friends who wanted to buy the trailer from us by assuming the loan. I made her the same offer, which she accepted.

After returning from Alaska, I found it difficult to concentrate on work. Mentally, I had already retired. I completed the projects I had promised to deliver, then rather than wait any longer to pursue my list of adventures, I formally retired at the end of 2011. I would have enough money provided I didn't overspend.

Graduations, weddings, and other events prevented me from completing any items on my adventure list during 2012. My elder daughter got married in September of that year. Seeing her with her husband at the altar, I contemplated their love, visible for all to witness.

On my Daughter's Wedding
*With this hand,
what you hold,
I shall hold dearly.*

*With these feet,
where you go,
I shall follow faithfully.*

With these arms,
what burdens you carry,
I shall share gladly.

With these eyes,
what you see,
I shall witness truthfully.

With honest voice,
I cannot promise
to keep these vows perfectly,

but know that
with this heart,
I shall love you completely.

In the fall of 2012, I decided to take on the Appalachian Trail the following spring. I needed time away from friends and family so I could examine my life, my relationships with women and to consider my future. Sometimes I wonder whether I had something to prove to Triveni, but I think not really because spite wouldn't carry one very far on the Trail. I calculated that it would take me roughly 200 days, or the equivalent of 40 five-day hikes back to back, as if I had been one of the gold-rushers crossing the Chilkoot Pass with their supplies. I had survived the Chilkoot Trail one-way, so I should be able to do the Appalachian Trail or at least a good part of it.

Foolish me!

Before I left for the Appalachian Trail, I went to see a priest. I didn't know if I was able to make a sincere confession. Frankly, I wasn't certain that I was sorry for some sins. In fact, I had rather enjoyed them. He laughed and explained that my sins had made me the person I was today, then asked if I wanted to continue repeating them. I replied, "No, I'm done." He then heard my confession.

Clean

You have traveled long, far, and wide,
hoping to find someone or something.
Alone you remain incomplete and unsatisfied,
anxious about what your future might bring.
What does it matter? Why should it matter?
Where have you been?

You have done deeds you can no longer bear,
things you regret but can never forget,
memories bring you sorrow and despair.
How does one end a constant feeling of debt?
What does it matter? Why should it matter?
What have you done?

Thoughtlessly you looked in the wrong places,
misplacing your trust and passion,
foolishly making friends with the wrong people,
and recklessly making love to the wrong women.
What does it matter? Why should it matter?
Why should I care? Whom have you known?

At last you have returned here to me
ready to leave your past behind.
All this while, I have waited patiently
for you to realize your place is with me.
What does it matter? Why should it matter?
Why should I care? Now you are with me
and my love shall make you clean.

In mid-March 2013, I left for the Appalachian Trail and stopped in late May. Unlike the triumphant return of my friends who completed the Trail, how did my ending go? My family was glad to have me home. Most other people were impressed that I had been gone so long and accomplished so much: over nine weeks and 733 miles (including the approach trail from Amicalola). Some, who were more experienced at hiking and camping, had been concerned that I was ill-prepared; to a degree, these people were correct. However, they had failed to consider my ability to adapt. A very few seemed satisfied to have their expectations, that I would not complete the entire 2,186 miles of the Trail, confirmed. Going back to the Trail for another eight weeks in 2014, however, appeared to cause them to concede my resolve and resilience.

When prospective trekkers ask what advice I might give them, I caution them that I am not the best person to ask, having left the trail early three times in two years, but this is what I tell them. "Hike cold; sleep warm; drink all the water you can before leaving a spring; drink extra calories; buy the foods you want to eat locally and take more zero days than you think you need. You wouldn't last long working more than 40 hours a week at a physically demanding job. What makes you think you can hike more than that week after week?"

For those hikers receptive to it, the Trail encourages personal growth.

Through-hikers had told me that I would experience a period of decompression after I left the Trail. I would want to talk about my experience, but people would quickly tire of my stories. Even the best of my friends would finally have had enough. They would want to talk about other things more important to them. Fortunately, I struck up a friendship with a young through-hiker who lives near me. We meet once in a while to talk about our experiences over breakfast. I found another release for my stories when I started to write this book.

Veteran trekkers had said that the experience would change me. Friends and family would notice a difference, but would not understand it, because their world hadn't changed.

How had the Trail influenced me? I returned a better person: kinder, calmer, stronger, more confident, and more certain of what I want from life. I'm stronger in my faith and values, although, I joke, still practicing in the hopes of someday getting them right.

In one way, it doesn't matter how much of the Trail a hiker completes. Whether one has completed the 31 miles to Neel Gap or hiked all the way to Katahdin, it is an accomplishment that few people would attempt. A person cannot help but be changed by the experience. Hiking the Trail reveals your strengths, weaknesses, and limitations, and forces you to cope with them. For those hikers receptive to it, the Trail encourages personal growth.

When I started the Trail in Georgia, I heard people criticize and mock a certain writer who wrote a popular book about the Appalachian Trail because he hadn't completed the entire Trail. At Springer, a man with a beer belly wore a shirt bearing a derogatory term for a weakling to describe the author.

Even trekkers fell into the mind-set that those who made it all the way were a special breed and the rest were not as worthy. I myself felt that way when I aspired to be a through-hiker. Those who completed the Trail deserve every bit of recognition they receive and more. It is an incredible accomplishment. They are the cream of trekkers: tough, resilient, and capable, but also lucky to not have had an accident, illness, or a family emergency take them off the Trail.

Shortly after I restarted in 2014, a young woman through-hiker from Ireland, 20 years old at the most, walked into my camp. Barring accident or illness, I am certain she made it to Katahdin. When I told her I was a section hiker, she seemed dismissive, but when I said I was going to Connecticut, her attitude changed. She said: "Well, that is something," as if I was somehow deserving of her attention because of the distance I was planning. We talked for a long time.

Her attitude bothered me. It wasn't the judgment in her voice that annoyed me; we all judge each other every day. It is part of life, judging people against our criteria and being judged by theirs. But there was something I didn't understand—and that was the lesson hardest for me to learn about the Trail.

It took me a while to realize that for that young lady, the most important thing in her life was completing the Trail. I hope she made it. For her and others, completing the Trail was an obsession.

There is a well-known Trail saying, "Hike your own hike." The source of my uneasiness was that I myself had accepted her judgment of what my hike should be. Although I hoped, planned, and tried to complete the Appalachian Trail, completing the Trail was not one of the reasons that led me to start the trek in the first place. In fact, by Daleville, I had accomplished the goals I had set out to accomplish: to reflect on my life and to try my hand at writing. Regardless of whether my prose and poetry are good, as with hiking, my writing will get better with each effort. Now, when I hike, I go hiking completely; my attention is focused on the hike. My writing has become the outlet for the inspiration that I experience in nature and from others.

I did take one more thing away from this chance encounter with the young woman. When I have a difficult time, I don't complain. Now I just say, "That was something."

As with hiking, it is with my life; the path I have followed seems clear now. If I had not married, I would not have the family I love. If I had not divorced, I would not been changed by the women I met and dated. If they had not changed me, I would never have gotten into a serious relationship and never would have been introduced to hiking and camping. If we hadn't broken up, I wouldn't have started the Appalachian Trail. If I hadn't started the Trail, I wouldn't have undergone the changes that Slim and others noticed. If I hadn't started the Trail, I wouldn't have found my joy in writing, perhaps for the rest of my life. I must create, I must write. It is what I do now: write and hike.

I'm not naïve enough to believe this path was preordained. It's the path I chose to follow at each step. If I hadn't followed this path, my life might not have taken the turns it has.

As long as I can remember, bits of music have been running through my mind. Perhaps I'll learn how to play an instrument next.

In 2014, after returning from the Appalachian Trail, I decided to go on a day hike and met a woman. There was something different about her; I didn't know what it was that day and I still don't. Was she really different from all the others or was it the change in me? I only knew that I wanted to learn more about her. I asked for her phone number, she gave me one and when I called, she answered. It really was her phone number! We went out and then started to date.

Never Thought (completed)
Never thought it was goin' happen for me
but I met a woman hikin' one day.
Although it's too early to say,
we're takin' it day by day,
I'm hopin' she'll stay,

because she makes me happy
and I feel lucky.
And, I'm tryin' to make her happy
and feel lucky too
because I want her to stay.
Yes, I'm hopin' she'll stay.

I want to be her only lover,
the one she chooses above all others,
because I don't think I could find another
like her, no, not like her.

My daughters say the difference about this woman is that I really like her. Even though we disagree about almost every major issue, I respect her and there is a kindness and consideration between us.

It's not certain we'll stay together; I'm not assuming that at all. There are serious obstacles long-term. Our lives, our slates, are already heavily written upon. Yet, we will be together as long as we want to be together. That's enough for now—and isn't that always the case with relationships? You will stay together as long as you want to be together. If it doesn't work out this time, I feel I'm getting closer.

As I write these words in December 2014, I am preparing to tow my trailer from Michigan to the West Coast after the holidays to be near her and see how it goes. While there and on my way and back, I will stop to do some hiking in Texas, New Mexico, and Arizona.

There is one more thing. As long as I can remember, bits of music have been running through my mind. Perhaps I'll learn how to play an instrument next. Learning remains my favorite activity.

If We Want It to Be

I remember when you first appeared,
I thought I never stood a chance
and when you went away
I thought I had lost my only chance,
but then you reappeared
and took me as I am.

I respected your hesitation
and need for assurance
but remained hopeful that someday
with affectionate persistence
I would prove my intention
to take you as you are.

We took our time to be certain
of what we both wanted,
not just for today but everyday,
not time poorly wasted,
until we made our decision
to take each other as we are.

Sometimes we doubted
whether we would stay together,
but we always found a way
and somehow came out better
by doing what we needed
to deal with life as it was.

We spend our time together,
doing our best to make the most
of every moment of every day

whether in the mountains or on the coast,
nothing else matters,
the way love should be.

Because it doesn't matter what you promise,
which fancy words you choose to say
or how you stage their production:
promises are broken every day.
The only thing that matters is
what you choose to do today.

For now we are apart again.
Not that we are lonely
or have reason to dismay,
we have our friends and families
and memories to sustain us
until together again,
if we want to be.

We shall see.

EULOGY

In January 2015, I was in Palo Dura Canyon outside Amarillo, Texas. The Lighthouse Trail was a fairly easy 5.7 miles roundtrip with a quarter mile steep scramble at the end to a ledge part way up the Lighthouse. I dangled my feet over the edge, enjoying a candy bar and a bottle of water. I never would have done that a few years ago!

I liked the challenge of the Rock Garden Trail better. The five-mile roundtrip took me from the floor of the canyon up to the rim and back down. Part way up, I found myself momentarily gasping for breath.

I imagine that is the moment my mother died.

When I left the canyon, I called my mother to let her know I was alright. She always worried about me when I hiked alone. My sister-in-law answered, saying she would phone me right back. Soon my younger brother called to say that our mother was on the way to the hospital, but not expected to live. My sister-in-law told me that when she found Mother in her bed, she looked like she was sleeping peacefully with her head resting on her hands folded together as if in prayer.

We were stunned and crushed. The week before leaving for the West Coast, I had taken Mother to her doctor. He said she was doing fantastic. I left confident about her health. We didn't request an autopsy.

At the funeral, my other brother spoke for the family. He is an excellent speaker and did a superb job, including a few humorous stories and some of mother's favorite sayings. He closed with something I had written during my 2013 hike on the Appalachian Trail. I hadn't been prepared when our father died and wanted to have something ready for Mother. I showed it to her inadvertently. She enjoyed reading my poetry to see how it was coming along. This was in a group of poems I had given her.

Eulogy
Have you ever read a book
that you were sad to see end,
a book so well written,
a story so well told,
with words carefully chosen
and characters you love
as much as anyone?
How you wish this book
could go on forever!
Sadly all stories must end:
somewhere, somehow, sometime.

Our sadness today bears witness
not to the ending of a life
but to a life well lived,
of stories worth retelling,
of lessons taught patiently,
and of love given and received.
Today we gather in testimony
to this good woman: daughter,
sister, wife, and mother.

"Moments Along a Trail" is dedicated to the memory of our mother.

Two weeks later, I was in the airport at Denver on the way back to Amarillo where I had left my truck and trailer. My brothers and I had talked about the change in my life that my mother's death would bring. No more phone calls when we had a story to share with her. No more visits, no more doctor appointments. She had been our first and best trail companion. We wondered whether we would drift apart without her presence drawing us together and vowed not to let that happen.

MOUNT WOODSON,
CALIFORNIA,
MARCH 2015

While waiting to board the plane, I spoke with a young couple. The woman asked what I was doing during my retirement. I told them about Alaska, the West, the Appalachian Trail, that I was on my way to the West Coast and how I hoped to travel around the country in the future moving my trailer from spot to spot. As we started to board the plane, the woman turned to me and said, "You are a lucky man." I paused for a moment, considering her words before deciding, "I am a lucky man," for reasons she could not begin to know.

Come Hike with me (completed)
Rise up! Come hike with me.
Some bright, early morning,
we'll go places you want to be,
do things you want to do,
and see sights you long to see.
Rise up! Come hike with me.

Acknowledgements

I thank all of those who encouraged me and whose stories inspired these poems: my daughters, ex-wife, family, friends, and all the hikers, hostellers, and Trail Angels of the Appalachian Trail—and especially my trail friends, in the order in which I met them: Cruise and Corn Dog, Photo Bomber, Lady, Susquehanna Slim, Danno, Otto, Olive Oyl, WetBag, Dreamer, Candy Pants, Waffles, HoBo, and Up Hill.

Trail friends forever!

I also thank my advisors who have provided invaluable guidance. Without their advice, this book would be a shadow of what it is, my editor Judith Endelman, copy editor Laurie Gibson, Claudia Whitsitt, Hugh Baird, Gary Dudenhoefer, Cynthia Buzas and Thom Somes, Richard and Pamela Smith, Timothy Damschroder, Susan Kornfield, Angela Sujek, Jim Edwards, and Cynthia Barnett for their input and, of course, Triveni.

Author

TOM BUZAS graduated from Carnegie-Mellon University, Gannon University and the University of Michigan. He taught at the University of Florida and Eastern Michigan University, before entering business.

He is the divorced father of two daughters.

Recently, he purchased a ukulele and a guitar. He hopes to complete the Appalachian Trail, if not on, near his 65th birthday.